PITCH

DOCTOR

To Marcia,
my partner in business
and marriage

PITCH

presenting to win
multi-million dollar accounts

DOCTOR

Neil Flett

Prentice Hall

Acquisitions Editor: Kaylie Smith
Production Editor: Elizabeth Thomas
Cover design: Steve Miller, Snapper Graphics
Typeset by Robert Gray, Charlestown, NSW
Printed in Australia by Ligare Pty Ltd, Riverwood NSW

4 5 6 7 04 03 02 01

ISBN 0-13-257478-0

National Library of Australia
Cataloguing-in-Publication Data

Flett, Neil
    Pitch doctor: presenting to win multi-million dollar
    accounts

    Includes index.
    ISBN 0 13 257478 0.

    1. Selling - Key accounts. 2. Selling. I. Title.

658.85

Prentice Hall of Australia Pty Ltd, *Sydney*
Prentice Hall, Inc., *Englewood Cliffs, New Jersey*
Prentice Hall Canada, Inc., *Toronto*
Prentice Hall Hispanoamericana, *SA, Mexico*
Prentice Hall of India Private Ltd, *New Delhi*
Prentice Hall International, Inc., *London*
Prentice Hall of Japan, Inc., *Tokyo*
Simon & Schuster (Asia) Pty Ltd
Editora Prentice Hall do Brasil Ltda, *Rio de Janeiro*

PRENTICE HALL

FOREWORD

Without the strategic insights, structure and discipline and, above all, the personal coaching provided by Rogen, and Neil Flett in particular, we simply would not have won our bid for the Sydney 2000 Olympic Games.

Garry Kingshott
Director of Marketing, Ansett Australia

Winning the Olympic Games for Australia gave all Australians a tremendous thrill. The general support of the whole of the community was a factor in the broad strategy of the Olympic pitch but, like all plans for business, their success depended on a focused team and a first-class plan implemented by people with proven expertise.

The commitment to any vision, be it to win an Olympic Games bid or otherwise, has to be unrelenting. In the case of the Olympic bid we all felt the same way as soccer coach Bill Shankley who, when asked whether winning a football match was as important as a matter of life and death, replied 'Oh no, it is much more important than that!' This is how it seemed to all of us at the time, and none more so than Neil Flett and his team at Rogen.

The professionalism and enthusiasm with which they gave of their time and service was exemplary, and a crucial factor in the winning of the Games. One of my mentors, James Strong, often spoke to my law firm about the necessity for every part of our business to be performed with perfection. He said that it was all the little things done well, rather than any single factor that ensures a successful outcome as far as a business is concerned. This was the attitude of the bid team, and so it was that for the final pitch in Monte Carlo we went to the Pitch Doctor himself.

As Neil writes in the book, he was very much a part of the partnership which helped to craft, massage and, finally, to polish the most important presentation that any of us would give in our lives. I am delighted to hear that Neil's success continues in the broad Olympic arena. The presently preferred tenderer for the Olympic Stadium had its presentation prepared by the Pitch Doctor's team—as did the selected airline operator, as did the bank for the Sydney Olympic Games. Rogen International has been appointed the official provider of communication skills to the Sydney 2000 Olympics.

I need to remember, however, that Neil's business is not just concerned with Olympic bids. Only three of the book's 21 compelling chapters are devoted to his involvement in Olympic matters. By reading the *Pitch Doctor*, all of us can learn of the wisdom, the guile and the impeccable touch that Neil Flett and his team have when assisting a client in presenting a case to win the business.

RODERICK H. MCGEOCH

CONTENTS

ACKNOWLEDGMENTS

This book is the result of a career spent in communication and selling. The ideas have been gleaned from a variety of areas but mainly from clients in the course of hundreds of pitches and presentations and from my partners in Rogen International around the world.

The Sydney 2000 Olympic Bid was the result of the dedication of dozens of Australians. The people behind the Sydney 2000 Olympic presentation:

Executive Producer David Mason—who was seconded from Channel 7. Throughout the pitch he steered script writers and film makers in the right direction. He also spent weeks creating the images which were projected behind the speakers.

Director Adrian Hayward of film company New Blood and Old Money—His company was retained to direct the four videos.

Roger Holden—Roger was the technical expert who ran the audio-visual during the pitch, coordinating the images and music with the speakers. With David Mason, he created a mix of moving footage and slides which were seen behind the speakers.

The trainers and consultants of Rogen International. Rogen trainers participated in the selection of Tanya Blencowe and in the initial training of some speakers. They helped work on gesture creation for the speakers. Rogen chairman, Peter Rogen, helped to design gestures and to restructure the Prime Minister's speech—without ever having met the man.

Graham Freudenberg, speech writer—Graham drafted several speeches and worked with me to fine tune and focus individual speakers.

The Communications Commission—Made up of marketing and advertising experts from top Sydney organizations, the commission was led by Greg Daniel of Clemenger Sydney, and gave advice throughout the process. Members were Wilf Barker, Dr Ian Blackburne, Bob Campbell, Ross Campbell-Jones, Mary Easson, John Grant, Alex Hamill, Warwick Hastie, Peter Jollie, Mike Kennedy, Brian Kirkham, David Leckie, David McClune, Don Morris, Laurie Power, Peter Roennfeldt, David Smith and Mike Wrublewski.

The Monte Carlo Presentation Sub-Committee—Greg Daniel, Don Morris and Donald McDonald gave direction and advice at all times, without compensation.

The Board of Sydney 2000 Olympic Bid Ltd—The Board gave advice and ideas as the pitch came together.

Australian Olympic Committee President John Coates, vice-president of the IOC Kevan Gosper, and Bid Chief Executive Rod McGeoch—They fine-tuned the speeches in the presentation to ensure that they were politically acceptable and of maximum appeal to the audience.

ROGEN INTERNATIONAL

In 1968 Peter Rogen pioneered Business Presentation Skills in New York, working with leading advertising agencies, then expanding to train key executives in a diversity of professions and industries.

Rogen's unique blend of acting, communication and business skills, created the basis for what is now Rogen International—a training and business communication consultancy with offices throughout the United States, Canada, Australasia and Asia, and more than 60 consultants.

Rogen International is a niche training and consulting organization, concentrating on business leader skills including presentation, negotiation, selling and media presentation skills.

However, unlike most training organizations, Rogen International has a unique difference. In addition to training and coaching, it works with its clients to help them apply the Rogen International methods to win major business accounts. In the past three years it has worked with lawyers, accountants, management consultants, financiers, merchant bankers, developers, computer companies and advertising agencies to help them win accounts involving literally billions of dollars.

Rogen International's hit-rate in new business, on behalf of clients, exceeds 82%.

Chapter 1

The Pitch of the Century

ALL OF US SELL. Some sell ideas. Some sell grocery items worth anything from a few cents to a few dollars. Others sell encyclopedias or computers worth thousands of dollars. Still others sell services like public relations, advertising, law, accountancy and banking—worth many thousands and often millions of dollars. And then there are some who pitch for prizes worth billions of dollars.

The bid for the year 2000 Olympics was such a contest.

Once every four years, somewhere in the world, a group of around 90 members of the International Olympic Committee (IOC) meets to decide which city in the world will host the Olympic Games seven years hence. Worth in excess of seven billion dollars in tourism, business and hard cash to the winning country, the prize increases in value every four years, and each time represents the Pitch of the Century.

In September 1993 there were five cities left in the running to stage the Games of the 27th Olympiad in the year 2000. Beijing, Berlin, Istanbul, Manchester and Sydney had reached 'the finals' and, on 23 September, each city presented its case to the IOC in a series of 40-minute presentations in Monte Carlo. The last presentation ended at 3 pm and, for the next five hours, seven billion dollars hung in the balance as we waited for the verdict.

That night 1500 Olympic volunteers and sponsors, hundreds of media representatives from around the world, and 89 members of the IOC packed the Stade Louis II in Monte Carlo.

The announcement venue was a giant indoor sports arena, and our chairs filled the centre floor between the tiered seating around the side of the building. To our right sat 200 Berliners, equally excited and nervous; to our left sat the presentation and support teams from Manchester, Beijing and Istanbul.

At 8.15 pm those towards the back of the hall, including around 100 Australians climbed up onto their red plastic chairs, and stood in expectation. They held hands—not whispering, hardly breathing, just listening for a single word—as President Juan Antonio Samaranch opened the envelope to tell the world which city would host the 2000 Olympic Games.

The 200 Australians in the hall were only a small part of the team that had put together the Sydney Bid for the year 2000 Olympics. Hundreds of others waited on the other side of the world in Sydney, where it was 4 am. Crowds had gathered around the Sydney Opera House and at the proposed site for the Olympic Games in Homebush Bay. All waited with the same hushed expectation. For some of the most dedicated Australians, the pitch was in its 14th year. In 1986 Brisbane had pitched and lost to Barcelona for the right to stage the 1992 Games; in 1990 Melbourne had lost to Atlanta for the 1996 Games. Others had given three and four years of their lives to the Sydney Bid, and some—like me—had volunteered their services for only a few months.

For the past 10 days we'd worked extraordinary hours as the bid team pulled together the final 40-minute presentation and the lobbyists squeezed the last ounce of support for the Sydney Bid. And now it was decision time, make or break, a single moment when the decision would dash or confirm the hopes of five cities.

At 8.15 pm we'd seen the IOC members come back into the hall after voting. We knew they had been locked up for hours, voting in round after round for either Beijing, Istanbul, Manchester, Berlin or Sydney, with each round costing the city with the least votes its chance to win. As each losing city dropped out, the IOC voted for the survivors until one city had a majority of votes.

Now the voting was complete. But not even International Olympic Committee President Samaranch knew which city had won. The IOC members were aware that the race had been narrowed down to two cities. Istanbul was dropped from contention after gaining only seven votes in round one; round two had cost Berlin its chance, having gained only nine votes. Round three saw the end of Manchester with 11 votes. Only two cities remained in the world's richest race.

All eyes in the room swung onto the IOC members as, after the voting, they filed into the hall to sit in a block of tiered seats to our right. One IOC member looked down to the Berlin team and pushed his index finger down the seam of his trouser leg. There was a frantic whispering among the Berliners, and their spirit collapsed. I'll never forget a young girl in their team. She looked across at me, her face filled with a mixture of disbelief and sorrow, and she began to cry. For her and the hundreds of Germans who'd worked for so long to win the prize, the race was over.

And Sydney was still in...

I watched as Australia's IOC member Phil Coles walked into the room. He seemed to be steadying himself, walking beside a railing creeping hand over hand towards his seat. When he sat down he crossed his fingers. Another IOC member shook his hand and patted his knee—you didn't have to be a body language expert to tell that Sydney was in the final decision. It would be between front-runner Beijing and Sydney. But still no IOC member, let alone anyone else in the room, knew which city had won.

The hall was filled with whispers as each team tried desperately to find clues in the body language of the IOC members.

Australia's vice-president of the IOC, Kevan Gosper, walked onto the stage. He couldn't disguise his smile, his chin was held an inch higher than I'd ever seen it during the time we'd worked together rehearsing him for his role in the final presentation. There was no doubt that Sydney was still in the race.

Two hundred Australians stopped breathing. President Samaranch stepped up to the microphone, the white envelope in his hand.

Now only seconds remained...

Earlier in the day in the harbourside pavilion known as the Sporting D'Ete, we'd watched as Sydney made its 40-minute presentation to members of the IOC and the International Sporting Federations. And back then, as the strains of 'Waltzing Matilda' had filled the hall, everyone felt the hairs on the back of the neck rise, and most cried openly with a mixture of national pride and nerves.

Each city's team had given its performance and answered questions, then had left the pavilion to sit in hotels and restaurants around Monte Carlo, killing time until the decision that night. Berlin had presented first and had used tennis player Steffi Graf to help put its case. Sydney went second, at 10.30 am, then Manchester, Beijing and Istanbul. No city was permitted to watch another present live, but we could watch on cable television in nearby hotels. It was a day of anxiety, of assumptions made and discarded, of wild guesses and of more than a little drinking.

For me the day had begun at 1 am with visions of potential catastrophe. Hours earlier I had walked to one of Monte Carlo's leading hotels to rehearse with the Prime Minister of Australia Paul Keating, his wife Annita and advisor Simon Balderstone. Both Mr Keating and his wife were key players in our presentation, but their final rehearsal wasn't to be. Monte Carlo was the penultimate stop of the Keatings' world tour, and it showed. The Prime Minister, his hands bruised from shaking the hands of friendly Irish people, seemed exhausted but, compared with Annita, he was full of health. She had influenza and seem on her last legs. She cancelled the rehearsal and went to bed. I wasn't even sure if she would be able to speak the next day.

From 1 am until 5 am I sat at my computer and wrote her out of the presentation. I combined what would have been her role with that of the Prime Minister and gave him her script to speak as well—in case she was unable to present.

Changing the words was one thing, but each speaker had his or her own set of images and music playing on the giant screens behind as they spoke. The visuals had been computer coordinated so that the images appeared exactly as the speaker said the words. By taking Mrs Keating out of the presentation, all the visuals on tape were out of sync.

At 5 am I woke Technical Director Roger Holden and we met at the Sydney Bid office to change all the visuals in case Mrs Keating did not show. By 7 am—just two hours before the curtain went up—we had a new presentation, not as good as the original, but nevertheless workable. As it turned out we had wasted our time, because at 8 am Annita Keating turned up with the Prime Minister and made the decision to go on.

Few people knew what she had gone through or was putting up with during her part in the presentation. She was nervous, sick and exhausted, and agreeing to speak was a courageous decision. She performed extremely well, and our presentation kept what I believe was probably its strongest single surprise—to have the Dutch-born wife of Australia's Prime Minister talk with pride about multiculturalism and the welcome which the people of the world could expect in Sydney in the year 2000.

That night in the hall, all those earlier fears were behind us, replaced by pure optimism—no matter how naive. Even though we were exhausted, the adrenalin was pumping with the decision about to be read to the world.

Beijing or Sydney... Sydney or Beijing? Both cities had wonderful bids. The world was saying Beijing. The media had said Beijing. I saw the Manchester supporters go flat. They had been tipped off by one of their IOC members. I was shouting, 'We're in, we're in!'

On the huge stage President Samaranch held the envelope at the lectern and made an introductory speech to the silent hall. Then finally he opened the envelope, turned the insert around and spoke the words, 'We regret that there can only be one winner. And the winner is...Sydney!'

I remember only chaos as every Australian leaped into the air. Chairs crashed, supporters with them, as we shouted in victory.

Disbelief, relief, elation—200 Australians screamed in unison. The then Premier of New South Wales, John Fahey leaped a metre into the air, dragging with him a bemused Rod McGeoch, the bid's chief executive. Sponsors, friends of the bid, workers and volunteers hugged and cried as the emotion and relief washed over them. Sydney Olympic Minister Bruce Baird may not even recall his actions, but I saw him run 100 metres from the back of the hall to the front, running over the plastic seats themselves, leaping from row to row.

I remember vaguely thinking how strange it was to actually hug and kiss Dame Joan Sutherland and Margaret Whitlam, the wife of former Australian Prime Minister Gough Whitlam, within 30 seconds of each other. What are the odds of that ever occurring in a man's life?

We rushed around the room, looking for the team we had worked with in the weeks leading up to the win—Director of Presentations David Mason, Technical Director Roger Holden, world champion swimmer Kieren Perkins, our 11-year-old schoolgirl presenter Tanya Blencowe, Australian Olympic Committee chairman John Coates, Kevan Gosper, Communications Commission chairman Greg Daniel, bid chief executive Rod McGeoch.

Sydney had beaten Beijing by two votes—45 to 43. In round one we had scored 30 votes to Beijing's 32. In round two we'd slipped further behind with 30 votes to 37. In round three we scored 37 with Beijing three votes ahead on 40. And in the final round we came from behind to pip Beijing at the post 45 to 43. If one less IOC member had voted for Sydney in the final round, it would have been a tie at 44 votes each. And President Samaranch would have had the choice of voting himself, or calling for another round of voting. Nobody will ever know what the result would have been if either of those options had been exercised.

And that, with all its drama, emotion, cold-blooded planning and wild aspirations, is what the pitching business is all about!

The sensations that we felt in that room, on the other side of the world, created the ultimate reward for the work—the tears, the sobbing, the screaming, the running, hugging, kissing, a thousand words spoken, none remembered. That elation on winning the Pitch of the Century summed up for me why any of us compete, why we pitch, why we put ourselves through the work and the pain.

For days afterwards, as I returned to Australia and got back to work, I would burst into a grin for no apparent reason. It happened every hour or so, and I bet it happened to everyone who had been involved.

The founder of the Olympics, Pierre De Coubertin, may have been wrong—it isn't how you compete that counts, the winning is important too. In the world of pitching business, there is no other reason for competing.

Chapter 2

Coming First

THIS BOOK IS ABOUT COMING FIRST, when coming second does not count. It's about pitching for big accounts. It contains tips that could help win millions of dollars in new business, and it holds the secrets which lead to moments like at 8.20 pm on 23 September 1993 in that hall in Monte Carlo.

The techniques and tips outlined in the following chapters take key ideas gleaned from years of acting as the 'Pitch Doctor' for organizations seeking to win major contracts, each worth many millions of dollars—airline advertising accounts, film studio advertising accounts, major audit accounts, law accounts, media accounts, sponsorships, huge architectural projects.

In each case one supplier is pitched against one, two or even 20 other suppliers. And nine times out of ten, only one supplier can win. The founder of Rogen International, Peter Rogen, calls it 'coming first', and he's right. In business there is seldom a second place.

To these organizations, major new business is their lifeblood. An organization which is 'on a roll'—winning account after account —is one of the most exhilarating places on earth in which to work. By the same token, an organization which is off the boil and losing every pitch loses direction and this can be demotivating for its staff. Talented motivated people like to work with champions.

Whether a new account is worth thousands of dollars or hundreds of millions, chasing it and winning carry benefits beyond the money. A pitching mentality stimulates your team and focuses your organization. A company that is pitching is an exhilarating place to work—positive change is in the air, there is constant tension and excitement.

Essentially, an organization today needs to do two things to be successful: it must retain current business and it must add new business. It is not enough just to win new business, if for every new account won, an existing account leaves. Nor is it enough to stagnate by simply running the same business year after year.

The new business presentation is, therefore, a vital facet of any organization. A leader grows by landing significant new accounts and expanding those that it currently holds. There is no alternative for a company; it must grow to survive.

NEW BUSINESS PRESENTATION

Today new business has become a science, using communication skills, selling skills, negotiation techniques and strategy. And yet, despite how much we would love it to be a fail-safe scientific process, presenting for multi-million dollar accounts is one of the most exciting, motivating, frustrating and sometimes deflating aspects of business life today. It is filled with subjectivity, decisions made on values which we do not understand, changing rules and fierce competitive strategies. We can put in place the processes for pitching, but putting in the magic is more difficult.

I will show you in these pages how to remove some of the frustration and deflation through planning and application of skills practised by the world's best. And I'll introduce you to the magic that happens in big pitches, when the whole is bigger than the sum of the parts, when 'something clicks' and a dull pitch becomes very special.

Many of the techniques were created by Peter Rogen when he pioneered business presentation skills in New York in the 1960s. These skills are taught in Rogen workshops in more than 20 countries. Other tips in these pages have been learned from clients, as well as from mistakes made, but hopefully not repeated.

Peter Rogen started business communications when he brought his Shakespearian acting skills to a New York advertising agency in the late 1960s. The advertising executives quickly realized the value of creative presentation skills and introduced Peter to a major client, General Foods. Peter created a workshop involving communication techniques, practice and exercises. From that point his organization grew internationally.

It was 1987 when I was first introduced to the magic of a Rogen International workshop. I flew to New York as managing director of my public relations company to attend a five-day Advanced Management Conference run by BBD&O, one of the world's largest advertising agencies. One session of the workshop was called 'Effective Presentation Skills' and it was delivered by a trainer from Peter Rogen and Associates. By the end of the session I was fascinated by the skills and techniques taught. Like most public relations executives around the world, I'd been tap-dancing for years, relying on my years of experience to overcome a near total lack of preparation.

Here were techniques which seemed to make an inordinate amount of sense—so much so that I returned to Australia and enrolled in a three-day Rogen workshop. I came out of that workshop and two days later presented for, and won, a piece of business worth around $200,000. And I never looked back.

Within a year I'd met Peter Rogen and purchased the licence for his products in Australia. A year later we added New Zealand and a year after that the USA, and Canada. With a wonderful team of dynamic young enthusiasts, we developed a training business which delivered the goods to thousands of business people, and has helped organizations win some mammoth competitive accounts. In 1993 we took control of Rogen International around the world and, with Peter, began to export the techniques to business people on every continent.

Rogen International is a unique organization—we not only teach business people how to present persuasively and with confidence, but we also coach companies on how to win specific business pitches.

Chapter 3

Sydney's Olympic Presentation

ROGEN INTERNATIONAL'S ROLE in the Sydney 2000 Olympic Bid was to train the bid's public speakers, to work on the speeches and their structure, and to coach the speakers for the final presentation in Monte Carlo. It was a very minor role compared with the parts played by others in the pitch, but it provided the opportunity to apply our techniques to a key part of the bid.

It may have been the world's biggest pitch, but it was nevertheless a pitch like any other, in which several competing 'suppliers'—in this case Istanbul, Beijing, Sydney, Berlin and Manchester—were pitching to the client—the International Olympic Committee—for a major piece of business.

There were some critical differences between this pitch and others, which made it very difficult and very interesting. For example, instead of having the usual number of decision-makers—normally from one to, say, eight—there were 93 decision-makers, each with one anonymous vote. Instead of the piece of business being worth a few hundred thousand dollars, it was worth seven billion dollars plus. And instead of all the competitors being alike, the competing cities in the final months ranged from the ancient city of Istanbul, through to the newly merged culture of Berlin, to Sydney with its natural beauty, safety and friendliness, to Manchester with its history, and finally to the incredible political power of Beijing, representing some 1.2 billion Chinese.

But those differences aside, this was a pitch.

Rogen International was selected to assist with the bid, initially in the rehearsal stage, but very quickly on a wider basis. We volunteered our services and, as bid chief executive Rod McGeoch said on appointing us, 'Your credentials check out and, besides, the price is right'. We took over the speech writing from Graham Freudenberg and prepared speeches for several of the key speakers. We worked with David Mason on strategy. We tried different structures and spent days reading speeches at different speeds while the Technical Director Roger Holden and David spliced in the visuals which would appear on the two huge screens on either side of the presenters.

Over a two-month period we coached the presenters in offices, in their homes, in convention centres and in hotel ballrooms. On one occasion swimmer Kieren Perkins was rehearsed in his Brisbane home, using a piano stool and bird cage as the lectern.

In Monte Carlo we kept rehearsing. And our role in the presentation was still minor compared with others. David Mason coordinated the presentation, reporting to a Communications Commission comprising some of Australia's top advertising, marketing, sporting and cultural experts. To a large degree these people, and others who served on similar Commissions on a voluntary basis, advising on other aspects of the bid, were the unsung heroes of Sydney's pitch. They worked for years without much public recognition and, when their work was done, they went back to their normal jobs.

Everyone's point of view was taken into account during every step of the preparation. The speeches were sent around the world to the president of the Australian Olympic Committee John Coates and to IOC members Kevan Gosper and Phil Coles. We faxed them to bid chief executive Rod McGeoch in hotels in Europe and Asia.

Each of the eight speakers played a role in critiquing their own speeches, because the words had to be their own. Simon Balderstone, the Olympic adviser to the Prime Minister Paul Keating and his wife Annita, reworked their speeches and sent them back for further adjustment.

And so it went on, until every word had been studied for its own meaning and then in relation to the other words in the presentation—a total of 2800 words in eight speeches, written in 10 different drafts—until they were as good as they were going to get.

Rogen trainers worked with individual speakers, as well as helping David run three major rehearsals in Sydney and one in Monte Carlo. Our role was to polish the speakers' performances and to put the best words in their mouths. The final presentation may have won crucial votes, enough to tip Sydney over the winning line. It may not have. Because nobody will ever know which IOC member voted for which city, it is impossible to say what won the bid. Personally, I believe it was the combination of everything which Sydney did—planning, audience analysis, attention to detail, sheer selling skills, strategic thinking and delivery.

I don't think anyone ever knows the real reasons why one supplier is appointed over another. As American industrialist JP Morgan once said, 'A man has two reasons for doing something: the right reason and the real reason'. Any major business decision tends to be made amid a flurry of conflicting influences: experience, circumstance, technical needs, politics, trust, lack of trust, rational thinking, emotion, cultural needs, desires. When the business is finally awarded, even the decision-makers have forgotten why they really made the choice, if they ever knew.

The objective of the Sydney 2000 Olympic presentation was to show that Sydney offered professionally organized Games designed for the athletes, staged in a city which personified friendship. Taking those key points into account, the speeches were crafted.

Here's how Sydney's Olympic 2000 presentation flowed.

CREATIVE OPENING

Presentations are delivered for the heart as well as the head. I talk more later about emotion and presentation, but a creative opening can play a major part in putting in place the theme, and setting a certain tone for the presentation. (More in Chapter 16 Making It Persuasive.)

For the Sydney 2000 Olympic Bid in Monte Carlo we opened with the room in darkness. Suddenly there was a CRACK! as a starter's pistol went off, and on the twin screens an Olympic athletics event started. The video began in black and white using original footage of the early Olympics. The objective was to startle and grab audience attention, the emotional intention was to underline the fact that, like only one other country in the world, Australia had been at every Olympic Games since they were first considered. Gradually the footage changed to colour to reveal athletes performing in more recent times. The background music suddenly increased in volume and the strains of 'Waltzing Matilda' filled the hall. I remember sitting at the back of the hall when 'Waltzing Matilda' began. In front of me sat 200 Australian supporters and as they recognized the music I began to hear crying, sniffing and blowing of noses.

I turned to David Mason and whispered, 'David, the Australians are crying'. He turned to me and replied, 'Yes', tears streaming down his own cheeks.

KEVAN GOSPER

Our first speaker was IOC vice-president Kevan Gosper, whose role was to formally present the Sydney Bid. (More in Chapter 15 Structuring the Presentation). His speech reflected a formality that suited his role as a vice-president of the IOC and matched the importance of the occasion. I wrote it with Graham Freudenberg, a speech writer for Australia's former Prime Minister Gough Whitlam. Graham's inspirational style was combined with my more down to earth style to create a form of language which had both the soaring tone needed for the occasion, and the 'Aussieness' which personified Sydney.

Kevan's speech made a simple transition from the video by restating the key point: "Australia and the World Olympic Movement have together grown from the very beginning, 1894". The tone and mood of this speech is set at a higher level, taking into account the need for a degree of pomp and ceremony. Graham Freudenberg's wonderful speech-writing style was maximized for this passage to appeal directly to the audience. It was not conversational at all, nor should it have been. It was formal.

It showed that we understood the spirit of Olympism and recognized the importance of the occasion. Later in the presentation we deliberately changed the tone to reflect the down-to-earth nature of the Aussie, but for Kevan, as a vice-president of the IOC talking to his peers, we kept the tone on a higher plain.

Mr President, dear colleagues and friends,
distinguished guests...
Australia, and the World Olympic Movement,
have grown together from the very beginning, 1894.

So it is with a deep sense of honour
—and an awareness of this historic, unbroken relationship,
that Australia presents the candidacy of Sydney
to host the Games of the 27th Olympiad...
at the Dawn of the New Millennium.

Our Bid is made on behalf of the First City
of a nation whose athletes have been fortunate enough
to have competed at every Games of the Modern Era.

And on behalf of a nation presenting its third consecutive Bid
for this greatest of honours...

Today we promise the Athletes of the World
a superbly organized Olympic Games
staged in a City which personifies Friendship
and the very essence of the Olympic Movement.

Australia's clear vision
is to create a platform of confidence, optimism
and harmony for all
which will project the Olympic Movement
safely into the next Century.

That is our message to you today.

I know that many of you already have an understanding of
Sydney's character and commitment.

And in the next 40 minutes we invite you
to again share with us that very special Spirit

> *which we believe belongs to the nature*
> *and character of Australia...*
> *—a nation as young and as modern as Sydney 2000*
>
> *—in a continent as old as time itself.*

As he finished the lights slowly dimmed and the sound of Aboriginal music filled the room. The second video began.

BEHIND THE SCENES

We used tactics in our speeches which were designed to ensure that the Sydney team came across as they should—genuine and down-to-earth. For example, I recommended that we did not use teleprompters for the presentation. Teleprompters use two clear panels of plexiglass positioned to each side and in front of the presenter. An operator sits behind a curtain out of sight of the audience and scrolls the speech in time to the presenter's pace. As the shuttle is turned, the words are projected onto the screens, invisible to the audience but able to be read by the presenter. The presenter looks from one screen to the other as he or she reads and the audience is fooled into thinking that the speaker is actually looking at them.

I didn't want them used for two reasons. First, the speaker's attention is not actually on the audience members at all. Contact is never made between speaker and audience. It stops at the words on the screen. (More in Chapter 6 The Role of Communication.) While it can be invaluable in making the presenter appear comfortable, it is nevertheless a con, albeit a clever one. Secondly, we did not want to make the Australians look 'slick'. We were conscious that many third-world countries look on Australia as being just like the USA; and given that Atlanta had won the Games for 1996, we did not want to be perceived as reflecting the 'Hollywood' values which could have been attributed to the USA by some voters. Other bid cities used teleprompters. Sydney used scripted speeches and speech notes, but with a difference.

Kevan Gosper's speech, like all those written for the presentation, was laid out so that each line ended at a natural pause point—at the end of a complete thought. This is a Rogen technique designed to help the presenter look down to his or her notes at a time when it could be expected that a pause would occur.

Most speeches are laid out by word processors that simply fill each line then create another. The result is that the page is filled from top to bottom with a square of black type. It is hard for the speaker to find where he or she is meant to be. Worse, because the line ends where the word processor decides, the line often breaks at the most inappropriate place, for instance, in the middle of a word, a phrase or a complete thought. So just when the speaker should be looking at a listener in the audience, he or she is forced to break eye contact and look down to find the next word. And because the break in eye contact occurs at an abnormal time, it is noticed by the audience and distracts from the message—just as it would if you were talking one-on-one with someone. By laying out each line as a complete thought, the speaker can glance down for the next line at a natural place in the sentence—where one would normally find a comma, dash, full stop or pause.

The speeches were typed in 18 to 20 point serif type, with double-spaced lines and the words only filling the top half of each page.

This kept the words at the top of the lectern, so the presenters did not have to look down too far to find the words—a necessity because Kevan Gosper, Kieren Perkins and Rod McGeoch are all tall men.

Kevan Gosper had been busy lobbying for Sydney in the months leading up to the pitch. He hadn't been in Sydney to rehearse, but in Monte Carlo he made himself available to rehearse with me again and again. I had been told that when he had presented for Melbourne's bid four years earlier, he had been thought by some to be lecturing instead of presenting. So we changed his glasses to full glasses, instead of half-frames, and had him raise his head just an inch, thus avoiding any sense of "talking down".

VIDEO: THE SPIRIT OF THE LAND

This dramatic video took the audience on a trip through Australia, from its Aboriginal beginnings, to its flora and fauna and wonderful scenery, ending with a panoramic shot of the Sydney Opera House. In a couple of minutes director Adrian Hayward gave the audience a bird's eye view of one of the most dramatic and powerful landscapes in the world. And in it were many Australian icons: Uluru, road trains, deserts, reefs, beaches, ending with a dramatic swoop over the bush to reveal a stunning Sydney Harbour, the Sydney Harbour Bridge and the Opera House. The Olympic rings slowly materialised from the sails of the Opera House as the music faded.

BEHIND THE SCENES

In the final weeks leading up to the pitch, this video came under fire from the Communications Commission, whose members (all marketing and advertising experts) felt it lacked enough Australian icons.

Communications Director Greg Daniel negotiated with the director Adrian Hayward and had extra footage edited into the film to show Uluru, a road train and Aboriginal dancers. To me this was an example of two key points in business pitching:

1. Always seek out the advice of experts.

2. Never be satisfied, because going that extra inch always pays off.

THE PREMIER OF NEW SOUTH WALES

As the first ring appeared from the Opera House sails on the video, the then Premier of New South Wales, John Fahey, stood up in the darkness and slowly walked to the lectern, arriving as his name appeared on the screens. His role was to make it very plain that Sydney would be ready in its infrastructure, funding and, importantly, in its attitude to the Games. The tone of the speech is factual, business-like and credible—full of facts and ticked boxes.

Mr President, Members,

I have the honour to invite the Olympic family
and the athletes of the world
to share the spirit of Sydney in the Year 2000...

I've never seen the people of Sydney as excited,
as hopeful, as enthusiastic
as they have become over the Olympic Bid.

Our city is filled with the Olympic Spirit.

*Our people have been touched by the Movement
and have given it their unqualified support.
Support which extends throughout sporting communities, business
and into all areas of Government.*

*As Premier of New South Wales
and President of the Sydney 2000 Bid
I confirm that if we are given this honour today,
the Games will be financially guaranteed
by the Government of New South Wales.*

*But my goal today is to prove to you
that Sydney will be ready for 2000,
not only in the spirit of its people,
but also in substance.*

*The natural setting of our harbour city,
combined with our substantial transport
and communication infrastructure,
means Sydney is equipped to handle
the needs of the Olympic family.*

*Our modern international airport
is just nine kilometres from the city centre.
With our additional international runway,
to be completed in 1995,
Sydney will handle
the international transport needs of the Games
with ease and efficiency.*

*We have 30 000 quality hotel rooms.
And we have already signed
a fixed price agreement
with the Australian Hotels Association*

to ensure affordable accommodation.

Sydney has a modern mass transit system,
networking road, rail and water transport.
Our transport system is capable of moving
800 000 people each day.

To carry the Olympic family from the city
to Olympic Park
we are building a new fleet of catamaran ferries.

Four of these ferries,
named after Australian Olympians,
are already in use.

Sydney has the modern communications technology
to bring the Games to the World.

Every venue will be linked
to the International Broadcast Centre
by an optic-fibre network
providing high definition television
to a global audience.

Health and hospital care
of the highest world standards
are available now and will be free
to all members of the Olympic family.

And all visitors will themselves be free
to enjoy a safe city...
a city which gives people freedom
to live life to the fullest.

Our Olympic security will be technically advanced,
yet unobtrusive.

Our Bid places great emphasis on the Environment,
and this has been further highlighted
by the support given to the Bid
by leading environmental organizations.
Mr President,
we were gratified
by the report of the Olympic Enquiry Commission
on all these matters.

Sydney will be ready...

—Our planning has been thorough and professional,
from the details of the Olympic Budget,
to the massive construction
which is now well under way.

—The Sydney 2000 Games
offer solid, modern infrastructure.

—You will have noted in our Bid Books
that the venues we have chosen
are on Government-owned land,
so they need not be changed,
unless a change is made at your request.

—We offer enthusiastic public support
and Government support
which rises above politics.

—And we offer a safe, clean environment,
in one of the world's most stable societies.

Mr President,
It's our harbour city's beauty
that we have used as the cornerstone
to build a very special Games Plan—

a Plan to create...the Athletes' Games.

To explain more fully how we'll do that,
no Australian is better qualified
than my colleague,
the President of the Australian Olympic Committee,
John Coates.

BEHIND THE SCENES

I had rehearsed with the Premier in Sydney and had several one-on-one sessions with him in Monte Carlo. It was a tribute to him that, regardless of the pressures of his position, he always turned up for rehearsal and took my advice on board. He said later that he had learned more about communication in the weeks leading up to the pitch than at any time during his career.

One of the realities of preparing for a major presentation is that even with the most thorough planning you cannot control everything. Two days before his speech the Premier developed a sore throat and sucked lozenges to fight the infection. I doubt if anyone in the audience noticed, but if you listen to a tape of his speech you can still pick up one or two points when his voice quavered slightly.

THE ATHLETES' GAMES

Having established that Sydney would be ready, the Premier introduced John Coates, whom many people credit as being the strategist most deserving of the crown of the winner of the Games. It was he who went to the State Government with the winning strategy.

As president of the Australian Olympic Committee, John built on the theme of the preparedness of Sydney by describing how the Olympic facilities in Sydney were built specifically for the athletes. He took the audience on a tour of the Sydney sites, describing each facility and the 'deal' for athletes and officials. John took a keen interest in the wording of his speech, modifying words and sentences to maximize the emphasis on key issues.

Mr President and friends...

From the time
that the Australian Olympic Committee
endorsed the Sydney Bid three years ago,
we have developed the closest possible relationship
with the Sydney Olympics 2000 Bid Team.

Together we have set out to make the Sydney Games,
first and foremost, the Athletes' Games—
a Games in which the whole environment combines
to give every athlete
the best chance ever to excel.

To achieve that goal we have brought together
the expertise of our National Federations,
including the many Australians
who serve on Executive Boards and Commissions
of International Federations.

Our aim has been to achieve
the highest possible technical standards,
coupled with thoroughly professional planning
and organization.

*And so today I am delighted to report to you
that we have received written endorsement
from each of the 25 International Sporting Federations.
In every instance, we have set out to ensure
that no barrier stands in the way
of giving the athletes of the world
a successful 2000 Games.*

*Under our proposals,
the cost of round trip airfares
for all Olympic athletes and officials
will be met by the Sydney Organizing Committee.*

*We will also bear the round trip freight charges
for transporting all yachts, rowing shells, canoes,
kayaks and horses
used in the Olympic competition.*

*At a time when the universality of the Games
is a very real concern to all of us,
we sincerely hope that this assistance
will help National Olympic Committees
to be fully represented at Olympic Games in Sydney
and to devote more resources to the very important
preparation of their athletes.*

*We propose holding the Games
during the last two weeks of September—
dates which suit the International Federations,
particularly now that so many are planning
to hold Olympic qualifying events
at the end of their normal competition season.*

*Mr President,
Sydney's advanced technical preparations
have been designed to build on*

Sydney's great natural assets
and physical advantages.

Sydney Harbour will be centre-stage.
The main harbour
stretching nearly nine kilometres
from the Harbour Bridge
to the Pacific Ocean
offers a unique opportunity and venue
for the yachting events.

The marathon runners will cross
the Harbour Bridge,
and run past the Opera House—
a spectacular setting for this great Olympic Event.

Close to the Harbour Bridge
lies Darling Harbour—
now a world-class convention and exhibition precinct.
with a modern Entertainment Centre,
theatres and halls.

In 2000 it will be the venue for basketball, boxing, judo, table
tennis and weight lifting.

The International Broadcast Centre,
a media village,
and a technical officials village,
will also be located only minutes away.

Our International Rowing and Canoeing Course,
like all venues,
is less than 30 minutes
from the Heart of the Games—
the 700 hectare Sydney Olympic Park at Homebush Bay
in the geographic heart of our city.

Seven years before the Games
we have 70% of our venues built or nearing completion,
all of them modern facilities designed for the needs of athletes.

The focus of Sydney Olympic Park—
will be the Sydney Olympic Stadium—
a brand-new, 80 000 seat sports arena
designed for the athletes of the next century.

And around it will lie the venues
for 13 other Olympic sports.

Our new International Aquatic Centre
is one of the largest, most sophisticated
of its kind in the world.

Also existing are facilities for fencing, modern pentathlon and
hockey.

And planning is complete for the Baseball Centre,
the 15 000 seat Colosseum for gymnastics, volleyball and handball
and the fully covered velodrome, with its 250 metre timber track
and viewing for 6000 spectators.

Our commitment to making the Sydney Games,
the Athletes' Games,
reaches its clearest expression
in our plans for the Olympic Village.

For the first time in Olympic History,
the athletes and officials from all sports
will be housed within a single Olympic Village—
including, I stress,
those in the yachting, rowing,
canoeing and equestrian events.

Athletes in 14 of the sports
will be able to walk from the Village to their events
and all competition and training sites
will be less than 30 minutes travel from the Village.
In a very real sense, this physical unity
will symbolize and strengthen the spiritual unity
which lies at the heart of the Olympic ideal.

And this unity will create an ideal environment
for athletes to perform beyond their highest hopes.

One athlete
who is certainly no stranger to performance
is our next speaker,
the world record holder
and Barcelona Olympic Swimming Gold Medallist,
Kieren Perkins.

BEHIND THE SCENES

John had been overseas during our Sydney rehearsals, but in Monte Carlo he made himself available to rehearse as required. He presented strongly and made sure that every key point received the emphasis it needed. At first he had some trouble coming to grips with one or two of the gestures, but amid his laughter he changed his style and did a thoroughly professional job.

AUSTRALIA'S WORLD CHAMPION

To this point Sydney's presentation had been a largely rational, very persuasive combination of spoken facts and powerful visuals. (More in Chapter 16 Making It Persuasive.) Sydney had ticked all the rational boxes in its presentation to this point, starting to build emotion gradually with the videos, but concentrating mainly on the technical needs of the listeners. Now it was time to introduce more emotion.

Olympic Gold Medallist Kieren Perkins had won gold at Barcelona in the 1500 metres swimming, and was the world record holder in that event. His role was to prove that Sydney would be the Athletes' Games, because Sydney understood athletes. I wrote his speech in a style which suited his youth and his Australianism— conversational yet respectful.

Kieren is favoured by being extremely tall, handsome and friendly. He was the perfect choice as a young Olympian. I created some very powerful gestures for him and had him place his hand over his heart while he talked about how he felt about sport.

Mr President, Members...

John Coates has told you that the Sydney Games,
will be the Athletes' Games.

So as an Australian and an Olympian,
I am doubly proud
to have been invited to be here today.

Many of you, I know, are Olympians
and so you know, as I do,
that a successful Games means a combination of things.

First, I believe Sydney will offer athletes
a special level of freedom, safety and comfort,
and a clean, healthy environment.
The weather will be ideal for competition.

We will be holding the Games
during the last two weeks of September,
our driest month, with low humidity.
As John said,
all athletes will live together
in the one Olympic Village.

What a great atmosphere for athletes!

There will be all the excitement of the village itself...
and a lot more.

If you aren't training or competing
you will be able to stroll to the Olympic Park
to watch friends competing in other events...

And we can all walk together
to the Opening and Closing Ceremonies.

We will be surrounded by friends...

and our families can also be nearby
because more than 10 000 Sydney homes
will provide accommodation free of charge
for athletes' families.

The athletes will be able to rely
on the professionalism of the organizers,
because Australia already has the expertise
and experience to host the Olympic Games.

Australia hosted the World Rowing Championships in 1990.

In 1991,
we hosted the World Swimming Championships.

And in the same year,
we staged the World Boxing Championships
and the World Women's Hockey Championships.
This year we held the World Youth Football Championships.

And, on top of that, we regularly host
rugby internationals, cricket,
motorcycle grand prix,
Formula One Racing, Grand Slam tennis
and many other major international events.

In fact, 40 world championships
have been staged in Australia
in the last five years.
It's a lot of experience in top international sport
and it shows that Sydney will understand
the needs of the Olympic athletes.

The combination of Sydney's natural environment,
the professional organization
and understanding the needs of athletes
will add up to a 'Winning Atmosphere' in 2000.

It's the same winning atmosphere
that helped me to become an Olympian.

And it comes from our Australian love of sport—
a feeling that sport is part of our way of life.

As his hand crossed his heart, the room darkened and the screens filled with a swimmer's arm dipping into the water.

BEHIND THE SCENES

Kieren was in training during the build-up to the pitch, but was nevertheless present at every rehearsal. In addition we flew a trainer up to his home in Brisbane to rehearse. On the morning of the pitch I took him aside and asked for his help: 'Kieren, I want to talk to all the speakers about how they can handle the nerves they'll face today. You've swum in world championships and Olympic Games, you must have some tips for handling nerves. Tell me and I'll share them with the others.' Kieren looked at me and said, 'Neil, I've never been nervous in my life. They call me The Iceman'.

Thanks Kieren! History will show, however, that Kieren had nerves that day. He told me later that he stood behind the lectern in the Sporting D'Ete and shook. 'My legs were going six inches in each direction, I thought I was losing my voice, I forgot where to look.' The interesting thing is that nobody in the audience noticed his nerves and they quickly disappeared as he moved further into his speech. It is further proof that it takes the audience a long time to notice nerves. You can be dying internally, but it takes a lot for your audience to remember or even notice your discomfort.

I trained Kieren to use his eye contact in a very strategic manner. (More in Chapter 6 The Role of Communication.) Three days earlier, when President Samaranch had opened the Session of the IOC in Monte Carlo, he told members that: 'At the end of the day the only things which matter are the Athletes and the Olympic Movement'. He went on to say that ecological matters would be an important issue.

We picked up on this sentence and wrote it into Kevan and Rod's speeches. Then I coached Kieren so that during his speech he would turn to Samaranch when he said the words 'understanding the needs of the athletes'. It was another example of how, in a pitch, it is critical to demonstrate to the clients that you understand their business. (More in Chapter 11 Rapport Building and Probing.) Playing back the client's own words is a strong tactic.

VIDEO: SPIRIT OF SPORT

The next video told of Sydney's love of sport. It covered every aspect of sporting life in Sydney—jogging, lifesaving, running, boxing, soccer, rugby, basketball, athletics, rowing—and it dwelt on the elation of winning and the deflation of defeat.

A GAMES FOR THE YOUNG

As the video ended, the room once again darkened and the lights came up on the lectern to find 11-year-old Tanya Blencowe (who had been selected from 120 children who auditioned on behalf of their schools) standing ready to speak, her head barely clearing the microphones. Quickly Kieren Perkins rushed up to the lectern and put in place a lectern step for her to stand on. She climbed up and turned to Kieren and said, 'Thank you'.

BEHIND THE SCENES

The 'totally impromptu' scene had been choreographed and rehearsed to perfection. It was created because Tanya was tiny and we did not know the height of the lectern in Monte Carlo. If it was too low she would look too old. If it was too high then nobody would see her. To cover ourselves, I had a Rogen International consultant, Bruce McLeay, make up an adjustable lectern step. It was plywood and could be adjusted to be two, four, six or eight inches high. We freighted it to Monte Carlo and during rehearsal we had Tanya stand behind the lectern to get the right height.

But we had to go further. Standing on the step, Tanya looked almost too tall to be only 11 years old. We wanted her high so she could use the big gestures, but we wanted the IOC members to know that she was a little girl. So we created the scene above so the members would first see her virtually hidden by the lectern and then standing high above it with her big gestures.

While at least one media personality accused us of insulting the IOC by using Tanya, she was far from a gimmick. Sydney's bid strategy had included a wonderful idea which gave the city a real point of difference over other cities. In conjunction with the New South Wales Department of Education, the bid had 'twinned' 93 Sydney schools with the 93 IOC members. Each member was given his or her own school and the children communicated eagerly with their member. They wrote, sent postcards, posters, video and audio tapes. They told their member why Sydney wanted the Games and why they wanted the Games. And when the 60 or 70 IOC members came to Sydney during the pitch, they were each taken to their twinning school to meet their children. The children sought their autographs, sang for them, danced and asked about the Olympics.

There was a need in Monte Carlo to take the members back to the time they had spent with the children of their twinning school, and remind them of these dedicated children waiting on the other side of the world for their decision.

While it certainly was not my idea (I wish it had been), Sydney had the children of the twinning schools write to each IOC member. Each letter was tied in a ribbon and left on the pillow of each IOC member in Monte Carlo the night before the presentation. It simply said: 'Please give Sydney the Games'.

For the presentation we needed to have one of the winning schools' children act as spokesperson for all the schools. David Mason and Susie Tuckerman from the Department of Education joined Rogen International trainers in whittling down the 120 volunteers to the final choice. Throughout the auditions the children had no idea of the role they could potentially play. They thought they would be doing promotional work for the bid, but had not been told about Monte Carlo.

We put those young candidates through the presentation mill. Finally we had it down to 20 children. As a last test we asked them each to leave the room for 10 minutes and write a presentation about 'Multiculturalism', or 'What I will be doing in the year 2000'. They then walked back into the room and presented from the lectern. We agreed on three finalists and I chose Tanya for her 'unflappability'. She was a cheeky, stroppy little Australian and she worked out to be a superb choice. Her role was to remind each of the IOC members of the bonds they had formed in Sydney and to impress on them that there were thousands of Sydney school children waiting on the far side of the earth, to hear them vote for Sydney.

I tried to give Tanya simple words, without affectation, reflecting her youth and her sincerity.

Mr President, Members...

My name is Tanya Blencowe...
You may be asking why an 11-year-old girl
is speaking to you today.
Well, the reason is that
I have a very important message for you,

from the children of Sydney and Australia.

Thanks to the Sydney 2000 Bid
and your visits to our schools,
children like me now know a lot more
about the Olympic Movement.

Three years ago, my school friends and I
thought that the Olympics were only about sport.
But, through our lessons and your visits
we now know that the Olympics
are about much more than that.

You have made us realize
how important the Games are to everyone,
no matter which country we were born in.

Sydney is a friendly city where
it doesn't matter where you come from.

We are all Australians together.
We eat together, learn together,
and play sport together.

And that's what the Olympics really means to me.

It's bringing the young people of the world together
to celebrate sport and friendship.

Of course I won't be young in the year 2000.
I'll be 18...

But I'm already a volunteer
and so is every single one of my friends.
Like them, I will do anything,
just to be part of the Olympics.

I've also learnt at school
how the Olympics are about protecting the Environment.

That's very important to us.

And we think a Sydney Olympics
would be a great way to show the world
how we can all care for the planet.

Thanks to the Olympics
this year has been amazing.

In April I met Mr Ruhii from Mauritius
when he visited Sydney.

And he told us about his country
and about the Olympic Movement...

My class photograph has been on the cover
of this Share-The-Spirit magazine...

Today I'm not in school in Sydney...
I'm in Monte Carlo!

And now it is my job to introduce to you...

the Prime Minister of Australia, Mr Paul Keating.

BEHIND THE SCENES

Tanya's speech was a highlight of the presentation. She memorized her lines so well that she could have delivered them without notes—but the risk of something going wrong made the idea unacceptable. She sincerely believed in what she said and there was only one sentence over which she expressed discomfort with the wording. In fact when she delivered the speech she only faltered once. She paused, lost her words, and like a true professional looked down to her notes and continued. Few noticed, but I certainly did. It was at the exact point over which she had earlier expressed discomfort.

REGIONAL RESPONSIBILITY

Tanya's introduction of her Prime Minister was an opportunity to stress the friendliness of Sydney. He had read his speech once at a rehearsal in Sydney, and then had squeezed in readings as he travelled.

Prime Minister Paul Keating was at the end of a gruelling world trip, through the USA and Ireland. The Irish had loved having him there and had treated him well—perhaps too well. He was tired and in the end I'm sure he relied on his experience as a presenter to get him through.

His speech was a powerful statement of Federal Government backing, blended with regional responsibility. It had been worked on by at least three speech writers, including his Olympic adviser Simon Balderstone and Graham Freudenburg, who while having written speeches for Prime Ministers before, had never written one for Mr Keating. It was delivered without pomp and with sincerity, a tone highlighted by the opening scene when he joined Tanya at the lectern and put his arm around her. Then, as she looked up at him he said:

If it were possible, Mr President, and Distinguished Members,
we would have liked young Australians
like Kieren and Tanya to do all the talking today,
because they sum up the really important things
—the special things—the Sydney Bid stands for.

(Well done, Tanya...)

The Sydney Bid is about the world's young Athletes coming
together, competing together, celebrating together
at the world's greatest festival of sport and youth.

The Sydney Bid is about the hopes and dreams
of young people everywhere
for a world of peace and friendship
at the dawn of a new century—their century.

The Sydney Bid is a celebration
of the unifying influence of sport.

It's a celebration of the true Olympic Spirit.

That is the message Tanya and Kieren bring to you today
on behalf of all young Australians.

They speak for Sydney, better than anyone else can,
because the 2000 Games will be their Games.

And that makes my task as Prime Minister easy.

From the Government and people of Australia,
I bring the message that the Sydney Bid
has the support of all Australians.

It is also my duty this morning to convey to you something of the
special relationship

which exists between Australia
and the Olympic Movement...

Of all the great Australian traditions,
none is more deeply shared than the love of sport—
unless it is the love of democracy and freedom.

It is no accident
that in a country where the ideas of democracy
and freedom and social fairness
have been bywords for more than a century,
that sport should also have an almost hallowed status.

Because sport, and most especially the Olympic Movement, stand
for these things.
They express these universal human ideals.

Australia's transformation as a nation
is marching side by side
with the transformation of the region
of Asia, Oceania and the Pacific Basin.

Australians are increasingly conscious of their place
in the region,
increasingly involved as neighbours and partners,
and proud to be able to stage the 2000 Olympics
for the region—-
all the nations of Oceania and the Pacific Basin.

Sydney 2000 will be a safe Games.

Australia's unique experience
in creating a multicultural society of remarkable tolerance and
harmony,

together with the warm relations we enjoy
with other countries,
will go a long way to ensuring that all Olympic nations will enjoy,
in safety, both the Games
and one of the most beautiful and exciting cities in the New World.

These then are the things which make up our theme for Sydney
2000—'Share the Spirit'.

Everyone who comes to Australia—
whether they stay for a holiday or for a lifetime—
experiences a unique welcome.

It is a welcome which Australia wishes to give
the Olympic Family and, through the Games, the world.

And it's a welcome which has been experienced first hand
by someone I'd now like to introduce to you—
my wife, Annita.

BEHIND THE SCENES

Other cities used their country's leader to start their presentation in a formal manner. We opted to have ours play a role as a team player, stressing the friendliness and egalitarianism of our country. Mr Keating was introduced by an 11-year-old schoolgirl and after speaking, he introduced his wife. His words were conversational and friendly, rather than pompous and stilted. Peter Rogen, Rogen International's chairman in New York, helped to restructure the Prime Minister's speech—without ever having met the man. Simon Balderstone then added his input.

A MULTICULTURAL WELCOME

The Prime Minister was joined on stage by his wife, Annita. Her role was to stress both multiculturalism and the friendliness of the welcome shown to visitors to Australia.

Thank you, Paul...

*I once thought about Australia
the way a lot of Europeans do.*

*I thought about images of beaches, koalas,
kangaroos and sunburnt faces...*

*But when I moved to Sydney from The Netherlands
20 years ago,
I saw how narrow my view of Australia really was.*

*Australia has taken the best
of what millions of migrants like myself
have brought to their new home—
and made it even better.*

*In Sydney,
attitudes, languages, religions, and foods mix easily,
with Australian friendliness and fairness.*

*The result is a rich culture
and a welcoming community.*

*I am part of the 25% of all Australians
who were born overseas.*

And mine is now one of 140 cultures found in Sydney alone.

We speak more than 80 languages in our city.

So wherever you come from in the world
there will be people in Sydney
who will speak your language.

In 2000, our Planned Cultural Program,
the 'Harbour of Life Festival'
will be the perfect venue for us all to celebrate together
the spirit of the games...Australian style!

And that means a spirit of friendliness and fun!

I have felt the same welcome
that Sydney now wants to give to you.

It's a very Australian welcome!

To everyone who loves the Olympic Games,
whether Australia is their old home, their new home
or their temporary home in 2000,
I can guarantee that Sydney will feel like home to you.

And then she repeated the final sentence in French and Italian.

BEHIND THE SCENES

It was a master-stroke when the Sydney Bid Communications Commission invited Annita Keating to speak.

She had come to Australia some 20 years before and still spoke with a broad Dutch accent. So broad was her accent that her press secretary Wendy Guest had to change words in the speech so that she could better pronounce them. I thought that a large part of her impact would lie in the difficulty she had with pronunciation of some English words, so I made sure we left the words '2000' in the script. She pronounced it 'two tousand', which I thought would prove to anyone that she was not born in Australia. I worked with her at Government House and gave her the rudiments of timing and eye contact. She picked up the tips quickly and, although nervous, was ready, until she was stricken by influenza and exhaustion. This gutsy lady went on despite how she felt, and nobody could have better impressed on the audience the multicultural welcome which they could expect in Sydney.

VIDEO: THE SPIRIT OF THE PEOPLE

The final video sold Sydney as a friendly city offering a unique welcome to everyone. It showed the people of Sydney getting ready for the Games and going about their daily lives, people from all nations sharing the Olympic spirit. As it ended bid chief executive Rod McGeoch was at the lectern ready to summarize and conclude the presentation. (More in Chapter 15 Structuring the Presentation).

BEHIND THE SCENES

An example of the attention to detail shown during the pitch was the use of a cathedral scene in the final video. The inclusion of this scene, made sure that those IOC members in doubt understood that Australia was a Christian country. Details like this had been gleaned from the constant contact which Sydney initiated with IOC members. (More in Chapter 11 Rapport Building and Probing.)

RESPONSIBILITY TO THE MOVEMENT

Rod McGeoch delivered the final message. I believe it was the most powerful speech in the presentation. I wrote of the thousands of devoted Australians who would wait throughout the night for the members' decision. This was the last speech and as such it aimed to lift the audience to a higher level, reflecting an understanding of the movement's needs. Again, the words of Graham Freudenberg achieved the rise in tone. Rod summarized the bid offer and assured members that Sydney 'will protect and promote all those principles and traditions which you have protected and promoted for so long'. It was a conclusion that left no doubt that the Games would be in very safe hands. One or two of the gestures used in Rod's speech were actually developed over the telephone between me in Sydney and Peter Rogen in New York.

Mr President, Members...and friends...

The next few hours will carry with them
the hopes and aspirations of the thousands
who have toiled to bring their Bids to you today.

As we speak, it is late afternoon in Sydney,
and the crowds are gathering at Olympic Park
and around the Sydney Opera House
to stand together throughout the night
to await your decision.

These devoted Australians have worked together
to firmly build the Sydney Bid on the foundations
of those imperishable principles of the Olympic Charter,
whose power has touched Australia as a nation
throughout this entire century.

They will stand tonight, united in their hope...

*Joined by the light of Olympism
which has shone upon them.*

*Tremendously excited,
yet humbled by their knowledge
that the Bid carries with it powerful obligations...*

An obligation to the Olympic family...

A special obligation to you as guardians of the Olympic Charter.

And an obligation to the world.

*Our awareness of the importance of this honour
has been highlighted today by the readiness
of Sydney's infrastructure, transport
and modern communications.*

*You've heard, for example, that in this Bid
our third consecutive Bid
70% of our venues are ready
or nearing completion—
all state-of-the-art, world-class facilities.*

*And we've detailed how these Games
will be the Athletes' Games,
with one Village surrounded by venues—
a Games where—for the very first time—
all the competitors and all the officials
will be able to walk together
to the Opening and Closing Ceremonies.*

*A Games with environmental principles so high
they have been endorsed by the world Greenpeace Movement.*

A Games which will free the athletes from concerns of safety
and will help them push the barriers of achievement
beyond their highest hopes.

And you've seen that Sydney is a City of Friendship,
where people from all over the world
live, and play, together in peace.

A city which wants to welcome you in 2000,
a city which invites you to call it 'home.'

Mr President,
Australia's loyalty to the Olympic Movement
has been unbroken throughout this tumultuous century.

In making our Bid, we've come to know
—not only the inspiring force of Olympism
but also the extent of the task which lies ahead.

It is a challenge which the people of Sydney,
and Australia, will rise to meet.

A challenge which we will rise to meet.
For you are assured that as part of the continuity
from the Bid to the Organizing Committee
of a Sydney Olympic Games,
we will continue to draw on the Olympic experience and expertise
of Kevan Gosper, Phillip Coles and John Coates,
and others in the Australian Olympic Movement
who have worked so closely with us.

From you, we have learned so much and, of course,
there is still much to learn.

But in closing our presentation,
we make you the promise

that a successful Games in 2000
will be our unrelenting commitment.

Our pledge to you today
is that a successful Sydney Bid will protect and promote
all those principles and traditions
which you have protected and promoted for so long.

Our fervent hope,
is that the choice you make today
will give Sydney the honour of delivering to you
an Olympic Games in the Year 2000
which will strengthen even further,
the glory of the Olympic Movement.

Mr President,
On behalf of our entire team,
on behalf of all Australians,
and on behalf of all the peoples of Oceania
we humbly submit the Sydney 2000 Bid.

BEHIND THE SCENES

Rod, a true professional, had rehearsed on every occasion with the team and, months before the pitch, had a lectern placed in his office, where he spoke with great sincerity to his office walls and windows until he got it right. (More in Chapter 18 Polishing Your Performance.) On the day of the presentation he was suffering from laryngitis and thought he would lose his voice. On the presentation video, you can hear it going in the final paragraph—but it didn't fail him.

As Rod concluded the bid presentation, he beckoned to the bid team. They rose from behind the head table and young Tanya and

Kieren waved to the IOC delegates. I had told her to wave at individual IOC members and smile, but I suspect she would have anyway, out of sheer joy. I remember her asking me during rehearsal , 'What do I do if they don't wave back?' I told her, 'Just act as if they do, smile and get excited'.

As she waved, the IOC members started smiling, then one or two waved back and soon there was the remarkably moving scene of a little girl from the other side of the world waving to the audience of IOC members—and many waving back in the spirit of friendliness which we had sought to show in Sydney's Bid.

It would be wrong to believe that the Monte Carlo presentation won the Games. As in any pitch, the final presentation plays an important role, but it is only one tiny step in the entire pitch strategy. (More in Chapter 11 Rapport Building and Probing.)

In Monte Carlo it took on a little more importance because it was generally felt by the experts, who monitored the likely voting trends, that Sydney and Beijing were very close going into the presentations. A brilliant presentation or a disaster by either city could make enough difference to change the result. But, as you will read, I do not rely on the final presentation to win any pitch. It is an important component of a longer pitch process.

Chapter 4

Lessons from the Olympics

NOT MANY BUSINESSES pitch for accounts like the Olympic Games—worth an estimated seven billion dollars plus—but the lessons learned from Sydney's winning presentation in Monte Carlo are lessons which every professional can use in business presentations every day. Some are more obvious than others. The following points provide some guidelines:

✦ Understand your decision-makers better than they understand themselves.

✦ Find the real objective of the pitch.

✦ Know what persuades—and what bores.

✦ Carry the audience with you.

✦ Maximize the power of the visual.

✦ Rehearse until it seems impromptu.

✦ Pay attention to the detail.

Let's look briefly at each one in the context of the Olympic pitch. I will cover them in more detail later.

UNDERSTAND YOUR DECISION-MAKERS BETTER THAN THEY UNDERSTAND THEMSELVES

It is important to understand your decision-makers better than they understand themselves. I will spend a great deal of time talking about this crucial facet of any pitch. (More in Chapter 9 Who Are We Pitching To?) The Sydney team arguably knew its audience better than any other bidding city. Rod McGeoch alone used up nearly five passports flying round the world meeting the 93 decision-makers who held the Olympic destiny of each city in their hands. He met most of them up to seven times. Wherever IOC members gathered, so did Australian Olympic Committee president John Coates, IOC member Phil Coles, IOC vice-president Kevan Gosper, bid chief executive Rod McGeoch, the then New South Wales Minister for Transport Bruce Baird, Lord Mayor of Sydney Frank Sartor, the then New South Wales Premier John Fahey and dozens of other hand-picked Sydney team members.

They were there to find the individual needs of each member—just as you should do in pitching for any piece of business. You must do two things to get honest, clean, important information from the decision-makers: build rapport and probe. You build rapport so they want to answer your questions. You probe to find their real needs and guiding values.(See Chapter 11 Rapport Building and Probing.)

Sydney team members built a rapport with the IOC and, as a result, they were able to get more genuine answers to the real questions. Because of this time-consuming audience analysis the pitch message could be specifically adapted to influence individual IOC members. (More in Chapter 16 Making It Persuasive.)

Audience analysis should be an integral part of any business presentation. There is a simple set of rules to follow:

✦   Never present to people you do not know.

✦   Get to know each individual in the audience.

✦   Know if his or her role is as a decision-maker or as an influencer.

✦   Know his or her level of knowledge of your subject.

✦ Know each individual's style.

✦ Know what he or she values, rationally, emotionally and politically.

✦ Know what turns the listener on—and off.

This is not *an* important part of pitching business—it is *the* important part. Chapter 11, Rapport Building and Probing, covers the subject of audience analysis in more detail.

FIND THE REAL OBJECTIVE OF THE PITCH

Most business presenters go into a pitch believing the only objective is to win. There are actually key objectives for every part of the pitch process. Objective setting is an art because once the real objective is found, the rest is detail.

In Monte Carlo setting the presentation objective would appear at first glance to have been pretty clear-cut—just get them all to vote for Sydney. But the reality was that some would never vote for Sydney and, alarmingly, around two-thirds of the audience would vote for another city as their first choice.

Sydney's objective, therefore, was to hold the votes we thought we would get in round one, while trying to get the second and third votes of those who would first vote for another city in the early rounds. Once that was understood, a rather different presentation objective was required.

Given that most of the voters would prefer a city other than Sydney to win, our presentation had to be specially formed to achieve a secondary goal. Images of Sydney had to stay in the memories of each voter throughout the voting process. It was felt that many IOC members would go into the voting room with their favourite choice firmly entrenched in their minds. But who would they vote for when their first choice was eliminated? So one objective of the presentation—along with confirming those votes already for Sydney—was to make sure that when the IOC members' first choice city was knocked out, they would remember Sydney before any other city.

We pictured the members sitting in the voting room, having been told that their first option had received the least number of votes, and was therefore out of the running. Hopefully they would think back to earlier in the day when they had watched each city make its presentation. Our objective was to create very strong visual images in the Sydney presentation—images which would serve as triggers to emotions which we felt the IOC members had. These images would spring into the minds of IOC members as they thought about who to vote for next. Some were built into the videos used during the presentation. Others were created by the speakers—we had Kieren place his hand over his heart as he spoke of sport being a part of the Australian way of life; we had Tanya Blencowe lift her arms up to the sky as she told them she had a message for all of them; we stood our Prime Minister at the lectern with Tanya while he spoke the words which Graham Freudenberg had written:

If it were possible, Mr President, and Distinguished Members,
we would have liked young Australians
like Kieren and Tanya, to do all the talking today,
because they sum up the really important things
—the special things—the Sydney Bid stands for.

And, finally, we had Tanya and Kieren wave to the IOC members at the end of the presentation to stress the reality of Sydney people's warmth. Understanding the *real* presentation objective enabled us to tailor the words, images and music to have the maximum impact on the audience.

In some pitches the presentation does not play a major role. I'm an avid believer that the presentation should not be a new business winner in its own right, but rather a confirmation that the right choice has already been made in the minds of the decision-makers. Pitches are won before the presentation—it should be proof that the right choice has been made.

The lesson for anyone pitching for new business is to have the objective of winning the pitch at any time from first contact. You should be trying to ensure that, if you do have to present as part of the process, then you are presenting to an audience that is already on your side or at least predisposed to you and your organization. If you have to go to the final shootout, make sure you understand exactly what your presentation must achieve and can achieve. Ask yourself: 'What do I want each person in the audience to do as a result of the presentation?' Do I want immediate approval of a recommendation? Is that possible? Do I want to get on their short-list? Do I want another meeting?

Set a clear, attainable objective. Too often organizations try to get an audience to do something which simply cannot be achieved at that time. And more often, nobody thinks of a specific objective for the presentation, and the result is a meandering list of words and images, which sail right over the heads of the audience like a rudderless ship.

KNOW WHAT PERSUADES—AND WHAT BORES

We buy with our hearts and rationalize the purchase in our heads. A winning pitch team must understand this. Most of the presentations that I am invited to work on are simply too technical, rational, and too feature-driven. The key is to turn features into messages that go straight to the heart of the listener, tapping into feelings and beliefs which you, as the presenter, know are embedded therein.

But it is just as critical to back these emotional messages with real facts, so when you have won the pitch and the decision-makers are asked why they voted for you, they can give a rational answer as well. In advertising it's called 'giving them permission to believe'. (More in Chapter 16 Making It Persuasive.)

In Monte Carlo the message was tailored to highlight the major selling benefits of the Sydney offer. Again and again the words and images of the Monte Carlo presentation demonstrated that Sydney would offer a superbly organized, environmentally aware Games, which would be designed for the athletes and held in a city which personified friendliness and safety.

Look at this example of the blend of technical and emotional persuasive messages: Annita Keating showed Sydney was multicultural by quoting the facts that 25% of all Australians were born overseas, that Sydney has 140 different cultures which speak more than 80 languages. The benefit was stated clearly—no matter which country you are from, there will be people in Sydney who speak your language. But that was less than half her message. While the spoken facts were important, even more convincing was her accent and the imagery which filled the screen above her head. The visuals showed friendly people, sunny weather, multiculturalism, sports-loving citizens.

Sydney used facts, statistics, examples, analogies, strong visuals and testimonials to put its case. But it also used imagery and music to underpin the words being spoken, adding another dimension of influence.

The words were crafted to deliver benefits to the IOC, benefits backed with hard evidence, rational evidence, emotional evidence. But it was the pictures of Sydney and Australia, the music and the actions of the presenters themselves, especially Kieren, Tanya and Annita, that really convinced.

Let's transfer the above example to a traditional business pitch. If you have analysed your audience and set the objectives, your next step in preparing the presentation is to collect the evidence you need. This should be made up of the most persuasive set of facts, statistics, testimonials, case studies, analogies and examples you can find to do the job.

Because you understand the individuals in your audience, you will understand how they will react to your presentation. This enables you to tailor your persuasive message to have the maximum impact on them.

That persuasive message, however, will not simply be spoken, it will be heard, seen—and if really effective—felt.

CARRY THE AUDIENCE WITH YOU

The best presenters take the listeners by the hand and walk them through the presentation, showing them the wonders along the way, until at the end they have sold their message to the listeners. (More in Chapter 15 Structuring the Presentation.)

In Monte Carlo we used a simple but powerful presentation structure—grab their attention, make the offer, state the issues you will cover, deal with each issue, summarize and close. We had no need for opening remarks because both the audience and the presenters knew how the session would run, and President Samaranch had made the necessary introductions.

Our creative opening was a starter's pistol going off in the darkness, which tied in with the short video showing Australia's history with the Games. Kevan Gosper stated our offer and outlined the key areas we would cover: professional organization, a Games for the athletes, friendliness and safety.

Premier Fahey gave details of the professionalism which the State of New South Wales would display, the readiness of Sydney's transport, accommodation, funding and infrastructure—the building blocks for our proficient organization.

John Coates continued with the theme of professionalism and showed how it would apply specifically to the athletes. He detailed how the facilities would be the best the athletes had ever seen. His tour of Sydney's facilities again emphasized professional organization, and made it plain that the Sydney Games would be the Athletes' Games.

Kieren Perkins demonstrated that Sydney understood the needs of athletes. He used evidence to show that we had experience in organizing major sporting events to prove we could do it again.

Tanya Blencowe spoke of Sydney's children, who had already learned a lot about the Olympics and wanted to learn more. She talked about friendliness and safety and awareness of the environment.

Prime Minister Keating showed that Sydney had his Federal Government's backing and emphasized that Sydney would run the Games on behalf of Oceania.

Annita's message hammered home goodwill to all races and offered a welcome which would be given to the world.

Rod McGeoch's powerful summary and conclusion recapped the key points the Sydney speakers had made during the 40 minutes, then made the promise that Sydney would look after the Olympic flame. 'Our pledge to you today is that a successful Sydney Bid will protect and promote all those principles and traditions which you have protected and promoted for so long...'

This simple presentation structure is just of one of many available to your presentation team: grab attention with a creative opening, state your subject, give an agenda, cover each issue, summarize the key points made, then reach a powerful conclusion and make a call to action.

At Rogen International there are 12 different presentation structures, each most appropriate for a specific audience and dependent on content. The audience, the objective and the amount and type of information will govern your choice of structure.

Whatever the right structure is, the medium *is* the message. Your structure can be dramatic, keeping the listeners on the edge of their seats while they wait for the recommendation, or it can be bold and challenging. It can be reassuring or upsetting. How you release the information is going to have an effect on your audience, and anything that affects your listeners is something which warrants your closest attention.

MAXIMIZE THE POWER OF THE VISUAL

The videos in Monte Carlo were designed to achieve specific objectives. The first was a creative opening showing Australia's unbroken Olympic tradition; the second showed the Spirit of the Land; the third the Spirit of Sport; and the fourth the Spirit of the People. Each was superbly designed to touch the hearts of the audience and to work on the emotions, while the words covered the rational side of the argument.

REHEARSE UNTIL IT SEEMS IMPROMPTU

That sounds an odd thing to say, but it is possible to practise just enough for the audience to notice that you have rehearsed. The goal of rehearsal should be naturalness, and the path to being natural often wends its way through discomfort. The error is to believe that, without rehearsal, your presenters will be more natural. The reality is that they will be nervous, hesitant, unfocused, and their message will be lost in a sea of distractions.

The importance of rehearsal cannot be overestimated. (More in Chapter 18 Polishing Your Performance). When Sydney's team arrived in Monte Carlo for the only dress rehearsal allowed in the Sporting D'Ete, the team was ready. In the three hours allocated for each city to rehearse, Sydney completed two full rehearsals and then spent extra time fine-tuning and doing communication exercises.

The reason it was able to run two full rehearsals was because the Sydney team had built a replica of the Monte Carlo venue three times in Sydney in the months leading up to the presentation. Once at the Sydney Convention Centre and twice in the Sheraton Wentworth Hotel ballroom, the Bid team had created the Sporting D'Ete. Every detail of the Monte Carlo room was built into the rehearsal rooms: the head table, the screens, the speakers' table, the seating. And in between each major rehearsal, Rogen International trainers worked with the speakers one-on-one. By the time our team hit Monte Carlo we were ready for our fourth rehearsal.

It is so easy to sacrifice rehearsal time for other purposes. 'We haven't time to rehearse...it'll be alright on the day...it's more important that we finish the document.' The fact is that the winning organizations rehearse at midnight, at 5 am, whenever and wherever.

When clients tell me they haven't time to rehearse, it's usually a reflection of their lack of intention to win.

PAY ATTENTION TO DETAIL

The winning pitch team goes further than any other and focuses on the smallest details, fine-tuning again until it is as good as it can be in the time given. In Monte Carlo it meant giving extra attention to every detail. Because only 60% of the IOC members listen to presentations in English, producer David Mason had every one of the eight speakers' scripts translated in Sydney, so that the translators in Monte Carlo could not give the wrong feeling or tone to any word or sentence. Each translator had a copy of the script in English and then a copy in the language into which they were translating, either French, Italian, German, Spanish or Arabic. They heard the speech in English and they had the choice of translating or reading the translation. An added benefit was that if one of our speakers had said the wrong thing, 40% of the listeners would still have heard it correctly.

But even that degree of detail was not enough. To make sure that the translations were accurate, we had each speech checked by another translator.

And we went a lot further in attention to detail:

✦ We over-printed the name cards on the speakers' table to give them a last minute piece of guidance. Each card, on the side facing the seated presenter, had the words: 'Bright, Enthusiastic, Welcoming'.

✦ We asked the presenters to take off watches before speaking, because the lighting in the room reflected off the watch dials and sent a tiny spot of light onto the wall behind the speakers. It could distract, so off went the watches.

✦ Every gesture and comment passed between speakers was scripted and rehearsed, right down to an apparently casual pat on the back as one speaker left the lectern to be replaced by another. It may have appeared inconsequential, but touching shows teamwork and we wanted to show cohesion and camaraderie.

✦ Each speaker was cued by the preceding video or speaker. At a given image on the screen or at a given word, they would stand up from the speakers' table then slowly walk through the darkness to arrive at the lectern at exactly the right time. They would open their notes, compose themselves, and then speak.

✦ A tiny detail like the placing of Tanya's lectern step was critical. It had to be exactly in the right spot to allow the Prime Minister to later stand beside Tanya. So Kieren had to place it in such a way that it overlapped the lectern by exactly two inches.

✦ The speeches underwent 10 rewrites over two months, as the theme changed and it became obvious that different aspects had to be stressed or omitted. Phil Coles, John Coates, Kevan Gosper, Rod McGeoch, Simon Balderstone and David Mason all contributed ideas. And the writing continued right up to the presentation itself. As late as the day before the pitch, I wrote more lines for the presentation to pick up on a statement made the day before by President Samaranch when he opened the IOC session.

✦ We had even allowed for someone freezing or fainting from pressure on the day. Former Brisbane Lord Mayor Sallyanne Atkinson dress-rehearsed the part of Annita Keating four days before the pitch, and on the day she held a complete set of speeches in case any of the speakers froze, fainted or were unable to appear for any reason. (We told her that her brief was to allow enough time to be polite, then step over the body and read the speech.) Luckily no one froze or fainted, and her considerable talents were not needed in the presentation.

✦ The speakers were trained in what to do if they skipped a page of their script, or missed a line. They were taught to rely on the skills of Roger Holden and his computer. Nobody was allowed to look at a screen, in case it distracted them. Instead, Roger followed the script from the back of the room and drove the visuals with a shuttle on the computer. Key slides were placed among the visuals to allow Roger Holden to freeze on an image in the event that a speaker was going too slowly. When the speaker caught up, he would start the images moving again.

✦ All speakers were taught to deliver key thoughts while focusing on each member of the audience. Their eye contact was one-on-one.

✦ Because some 40% of the members listened in a different language, our speakers spoke slowly and clearly to make time for clear translation of the words. We built in time for translation when we created a dramatic pause point. Tanya's speech included the line: 'Of course I won't be young in the Year 2000, I'll be 18'. I thought it might generate some laughter and, then again, it might not. Tanya was told to pause for only a split second, then continue. As it turned out, there was a little laughter, but at least it did not distract her.

✦ Speakers were warned when the visuals behind might generate laughter, so they would not be distracted. As Annita spoke there were visuals of street theatre on the screen. We were concerned that if the audience laughed at the images, Annita might think they were laughing at something she had said. So we warned her.

✦ Each script was marked with gestures in appropriate places plus signals to show increase or decrease in volume, pauses and pace changes. When we had a paragraph that needed to be read with a greater level of energy, we drew a bold arrow pointing up the page to signal to the reader that they needed to boost their power. When a few words had to be read slowly, we drew above them an arrow pointing to the left and, when they needed to speed up, the arrow pointed right. We underlined every word that needed emphasis. We drew in pauses at appropriate times. Key gestures were signalled by the words 'gesture here' written in the gutter of the page.

✦ Nothing stopped us rehearsing. For one rehearsal in Monte Carlo the lectern was built out of portable display boards, stacked to approximate the height of the real lectern. In Sydney Tanya rehearsed standing on a carton of Corona beer, which just happened to be the right size.

✦ David Mason and I met often to brainstorm worst-case scenarios, ranging from power failure, equipment breakdown and loss of sound, to a presenter collapsing (a Chinese woman presenter had fainted in a Berlin presentation for the Paralympics.)

✦ All speakers were told to trust their script, and not vary from it. I told them, 'When you are speaking live to an audience like this, shooting for a seven billion dollars prize, it's not a great time for an impromptu thought'. As it turned out Tanya did lose her place, but she reacted by pausing, looking down at the page and continuing. The way we had laid out her speech ensured it was very quick to find the place.

✦ Some speakers had their own image on screen as they spoke, and others had images underlining the points they were making. The footage and slides for these images were chosen by David Mason and Roger Holden, then I read each speech again and again to find the exact timing of each sentence, so the footage could be cut to match exactly. Each speaker was then trained to deliver those passages at the correct speed. Three speeches had no visuals to allow last minute additions to script.

These are just a few of the details involved in the Sydney 2000 Olympic Bid presentation. Winning presentations tend to entail sheer sweat and attention to the tiniest aspect of the communication. The following non-Olympic example demonstrates the importance of attention to detail.

I once pitched a piece of business to win the public relations account for a large liquor importer. After he had appointed us, I asked for a meeting to find out why we had beaten the other companies. Was it our creative product? 'No, X was more creative.' Was it our strategy? 'No.' Was it our account management? 'No, that was no better than the other suppliers.' What was it? 'Well, when I drove into your car park yesterday for the final presentation, you had screwed a brass nameplate onto the wall over your visitor car spot, and it had my name engraved on it. That's what won you the business.' Attention to detail. Going further than your competitors. Demonstrating how much you really want the account.

When preparing your own business presentation for clients or potential clients, *always* go one step further than your competition. It may mean binding the proposal in a classy or spectacular fashion. It may mean staging a mini-show to grab attention. Attention to detail shows the client that you are professional. If you present in a superbly controlled manner, with great attention to detail, then the client is likely to perceive that you will run their account the same way.

The lessons of audience analysis, objective setting, structure, strong visual aids and powerful presenters hold true for all pitches, whatever the amount involved.

Chapter 5

Getting
Roll
on a

A STUDY WAS CONDUCTED by Peter Rogen over many years on the differences between organizations that consistently won new business pitches, and those that did not. He limited it to the advertising agency industry, but the findings were just as relevant to any professional organization that survived by pitching for major accounts.

There were a number of features the winners shared. I have summed these up in 16 points.

1. Successful organizations had a leader with a clear vision of what the company could become in three to four years. The study showed that this vision could be so strong that the leader could picture the company at that time, its people, its positioning, its products and its profitability.

2. The leader had an extremely strong level of intention—a desire to get there and a sense of urgency to make it happen sooner rather than later.

3. The study showed that an effective leader built a team of three to four people who shared the vision and had the same high set of values. Not only did these people share these values, but they expounded them persuasively to the rest of the team.

4. The team's first priority was always the standard of present work for clients. This is a valuable insight for anyone getting on a roll. Not only does most new business flow from existing clients in one way or another, but the client base must be strong and solid to enable the diverting of team effort to new business.

5. A new business plan was then formulated which had:

    (a) a philosophy;

(b) goals;

(c) honest acceptance of strengths and weaknesses;

(d) criteria for prospective clients (see Chapter 7);

(e) key prospects (see Chapter 7);

(f) key people assigned to key prospects. By allocating team members to 'tag' prospects, organizations were ready when a pitch occurred. There was at least one key person in the team already familiar with the prospect's business, problems and opportunities. It was not a last minute rush to research the business in a week; and

(g) resources allocated.

6. There was a consistency among the team on the positioning of the organization.

7. Pre-pitch work was consistently solid, for example, creation of a brand positioning through advertising and public relations, or the establishment of contacts.

8. The new business pitch had a theme.

9. Rehearsals for all presentations occurred without fail. Some organizations would rehearse after work and at weekends. In some cases the organizations would lock up their pitch team for three days of solid rehearsal.

10. The whole organization was involved in new business, brain-storming, sharing ideas, contacts, etc.

11. Key people on the team had built up a new business library. These files were filled with everything to do with prospects: their industry magazines, press clippings, videos and profiles. The files were updated constantly as new information arrived about prospects.

12. The promise of top management involvement was put in a most convincing way. Suffice to say that most prospects doubt the claim that your top people will stay involved. They fear— and often for good reason—that your CEO will land the business, then within days, their account will be serviced by one of the less experienced members of staff. During a pitch the top presenters may be present, but for how long will they stay involved? What are the day-to-day workers like? The ability to satisfy the prospect of the appropriate level of involvement is an important part of a pitch.

13. A 'team' of presenters was used. I am a firm believer that the depth of an organization can be judged by the level of presentation skills within the company. When a supplier has only one or two strong members on its management team, they tend to handle all the presentations. Most small organizations only have one or two key presenters.

   But a company with management depth also has many who can present persuasively. The client's view of the supplier's size and depth is frequently judged by the number of presenters they see.

14. The study showed that the new business team created a minimum of two presentations which could be tailored for different clients. One version would be 60 to 80 minutes and there would also be a shorter version of 10 to 20 minutes. These would be flexible, but standard. The point is not to reinvent the wheel each time. The team can become good at the familiar pitch.

15. The team's new business presentations had a hook, that is, a memorable surprise; for example, the unusual use of visual aids, an unexpected presenter, the transformation of a room

or an unusual place of presentation. There may perhaps be no specific surprise, but the pitch was excellent in concept and content, as well as in execution.

16. The organization used public relations to publicize itself. It had a real plan to build the brand and put its name in front of the propects and clients.

Chapter 6

The Role of Communication

IT'S A LITTLE PREMATURE to write off humans as communicators. Computers may be making great leaps towards delivering forceful, persuasive messages, but nothing can yet come anywhere near a powerful presenter, with a high level of intention, dynamically delivering a superbly planned presentation.

The Information Technology experts may laud their machines and programs, but until a computer can raise its eyebrow in response to a listener's comment, there is still room for face-to-face communication in business. Until a computer can come up with an impromptu, insightful thought based on a question from the audience...until a computer can read a listener's body language...until...

The reason I'm stressing the point that pitching is not an inflexible process is because, if it were, then a system could be designed that would win every pitch. That is obviously not the case.

Usually I would defy anyone even knowing why one organization was chosen over another. It's one thing to know when a presentation has been a success, it's another to know what made it a success. Often even the decision-makers don't know the difference between the right reason and the real reason.

WHY GOOD PRESENTERS ARE IMPORTANT

As long as the pitch is subjective, affected by emotion and politics, then the presenter has a major role to play. Today, every organization which survives by winning business needs to ensure that it has a sizeable supply of top presenters. Sometimes it is not enough for the CEO to do the spruiking. A more sophisticated business audience now wants to know that the person who actually works on the account is also an accomplished communicator.

So in an environment in which clients may well judge the capability of an organization by the quality of its communicators, the emphasis is now more than ever on creating great presenters.

The roots of all great presentations—the elements that make the presentation flow, give it sense and the ability to build rapport, and that make the listeners react and do something positive—lie in understanding communication.

The *Oxford Dictionary* definition of 'communication' is: 'The act of imparting, the science of transmitting information'. But *effective* communication is more interesting to us. Effective because, if as a business pitcher you fail to cause an effect on the buyers, if they leave the room exactly the same as when they entered, then you did nothing. Your task as a business presenter is to make them agree, to make them decide, to make them change their thinking on a subject, to make them want more, to make them buy what you are selling, to make them hire your organization. To do that you must be effective. To be effective you must cause an effect.

FORMALITY VERSUS INFORMALITY

The best presentations are not one-way transmissions of information. They are *two-way*. Listening and being aware of the clients during every stage of the process will provide you with a flood of information that may help to find the real values of the clients. If I had to choose between a presentation that is formal and one-way, with questions at the end, and a presentation that is informal and two-way, which encourages the client to get involved and talk about things, I would normally opt for the latter. But life does not always allow such luxury. Sometimes the circumstances demand a formal presentation. On occasions we have to pitch to a committee and questions are forbidden in the brief. Sometimes informality is seen as demeaning. Sometimes respect must be seen to have been given.

So your communication style is usually defined to some degree by the environment in which it is delivered. And communication is not just what occurs during the presentation itself. As Peter Rogen says, 'Communication occurs when anything makes an impression or influences an attitude'.

Every communication and every contact in the process of pitching can have an effect on the outcome. The way your receptionist answers the telephone when the client rings, the smiles, the way you dress, the way you listen. Check them all from this perspective: 'Will this communication improve rapport with this client?'

Do not neglect the effect that *lack* of communication may have on the client. Lack of contact can create its own impression, influencing the client's attitude to you and your organization. And remember, effective communication is one-on-one. Individuals, not groups, will decide whether you win or not. The effect of your message will be measured first by each individual in the room. So your task is to hand each person in the decision-making process the message that you want them, as individuals, to take away. In a successful presentation each individual feels personally affected by the presenter.

New business presenters cannot afford to be one-way mechanical communicators. You must be aware of your listeners at all times, ready to react and change to suit the mood of the room. If you are unaware, then you will not know when somebody does not understand. You will miss the signals that show you are convincing people. You will not realize that someone is asleep, you will not see that someone has walked out of the room. Your attention must be on the listeners in the audience at all times; because, without the listeners, there would be no reason for holding your presentation.

These cornerstones of effective communication form the found-ations of the pitch. They will become even more important when we talk about delivery in later chapters.

WHAT IS A PRESENTATION?

The presentation plays a key role in the pitch and, as a commu-nication form, it has certain unique characteristics. It should not be confused with a speech. In a speech the speaker is usually on a stage and, depending on the style of occasion, is behind a microphone. I have seldom seen this done successfully in a pitch presentation. In a speech the audience can number in the hundreds, sometimes in the thousands. The speech is usually scripted and its purpose is most often to entertain, inspire or promote goodwill. Although some form of persuasion may be involved, having the audience make a specific decision is not usually an immediate objective.

In the same way that the presentation is not a speech, it is equally not an informal chat or discussion. In an informal chat or discussion the audience is, of necessity, a relatively small group. Informality is the key—sleeves may be rolled up, and comments made off the record with agreement from the others. Discussions often centre around explaining decisions already made or around obtaining and sharing different points of view. There is no clear assignment of presenter or audience roles.

Entertainment may play a role, but only if it helps to deliver the action which the presenter desires of the listeners.

The pitch presentation is a planned, structured communication with a specific objective. The roles of presenter and audience are clearly assigned in a presentation, although the audience may often participate. Unlike the other forms of presentation, visual aids are almost always used. A presentation is designed to persuade the audience to make a decision and commit themselves to a course of action.

This decision is often of considerable magnitude. In the business world, the jobs of the listeners may be endangered if they make the wrong decision; the future of the organization and the presenter may hinge on the ability to convince. There is, therefore, a need to tailor the presentation to suit each audience and, where possible, each listener in that audience.

Because the presenter has a limited time in which to present various ideas and materials, the business presentation should always be an organized product. To make a pitch more convincing, ideas and materials must be presented in the most effective sequence.

When a presentation has been effective, things happen: decisions are made, agreements reached, actions begun, products and services sold, contracts signed, and votes cast. These are the outcomes of an effective presentation.

Chapter 7

Planning to win.
Do you really want the business?

MAJOR NEW BUSINESS PRESENTATIONS tend to be won by a team of people with the highest level of intention, focused on the desire to win the account. The account 'feels right' for the team and they will do anything to get it. There is no consideration given to losing—that isn't even a factor.

When the Sydney team set out to win the Olympics for the year 2000, there was no time for anyone who thought it would be impossible. Bid chief executive Rod McGeoch always knew it could be done. It would not be easy, but it was winnable if the right people did the right things. Australian Olympic Committee president John Coates had the strategy for winning the bid and he knew it could be done. IOC vice-president Kevan Gosper and IOC member Phil Coles were equally sure.

To their vision they added like-minded people, highly motivated and prepared to sacrifice anything to get the job done. They chose for their team specialists in each field—and left them to do the job with a minimum of guidance.

The same level of intention is needed for you to win a major pitch. If you don't have that, your organization starts behind the eight ball. So, when you put your pitch team together, select the motivated self-starters, select the dreamers, select the people who love a challenge and are prepared to work to win.

UNDERSTAND WHAT YOU REALLY HAVE TO OFFER

In setting out to find potential big business, you need first to understand what it is that you offer as an organization, and then decide who might want those services. Many organizations are incapable of rationally looking at themselves from the point of view of a potential client.

To get the focus right, put yourself inside the head of your potential clients and then look at your products and services again. For example:

◆ Being the biggest supplier may be impressive to you, but when you put yourself in the client's position, what does being the biggest actually mean? Is the benefit obvious? Is there a negative? Perhaps it means that you are slow to react, or too expensive...

◆ Being driven by quality may be your focus, but the benefit to the client may not be implicit. From their side of the table they make think quality means sacrificing fast delivery.

◆ You may think that being 'low cost' means you are value for money. A potential client may simply think you are cheap.

Sit down with your pitch team and take a blank flipchart. Write all the features of your organization on one sheet of paper, then convert them into benefit statements for the client.

Do it in these two ways:

1. Speak the feature of your organization out loud. For example, 'We have offices in nine countries' and then add, 'What this means to you is...' and fill in the blank. (We have offices in nine countries. What this means to you is 'that you will have access to local knowledge regardless of where you are in the world'.)

2. Prefix your feature with the word 'because', then speak the feature and fill in the blank. For example, 'Because we have

offices in nine countries, you will be able to have access to local information regardless of where you are in the world.'

Complete this exercise until every feature of your company has been converted into a benefit. Now you've started to look at your organization from the client point of view.

WHO NEEDS OUR SERVICES?

Now you need to ask yourself more questions. What sort of organizations want these products and services? Who has needs which we can service with these benefits? Write them down on a flipchart.

Put together a master list of industries, sectors or individual organizations. You may decide that your unique blend of benefits suits organizations in the Information Technology arena, or multinational companies in the banking sector, or US companies operating in Japan. The list will be defined by the benefits you offer.

When we opened Rogen International in Australia in 1988 we defined our target market as any organization that used the presentation as part of doing business, and could afford us. It was wide-ranging, but our client profile today spans all industries and government. Needless to say, our master list of potential clients was voluminous and we needed to cut it down to a manageable size, with the best and most likely clients on top.

The master list will naturally contain dozens, if not hundreds of organizations. The problem is that 90% of them will not suit you—and you won't suit them either. You must qualify the companies on the list.

DO YOU REALLY WANT THE BUSINESS?

As a team, your first decision should be 'Do we really want this business?' The world is full of organizations that have chased a large account, won it, then regretted it for weeks, months or years. So the first rule is a simple, but important one: 'Pitch only what you want to win.' To put it in analytical terms, the benefits of winning the account must more than justify the investment and opportunity cost of pursuing, acquiring and maintaining the account in the short and long-term.

Some clients will be harder to win than others; and others will be lying around waiting for you to pick them up. Some clients will return solid, long-term profits and will themselves benefit greatly from your product or service. You will have a relationship that will grow profitably for both sides. But other clients will clash with your company culture, create non-productive work, drain your resources and your cash, refuse to pay, and dominate your daily lives to the point where other clients suffer. The opportunity cost makes the business a disaster. In short, you would be better off to spend your time doing something else. The next step will narrow the field to the most attractive and profitable possibilities.

Think about potential business from the following six angles:

1. the client's current needs;

2. financial aspects;

3. business potential;

4. difficulty of sale;

5. on-going relationship; and

6. timing.

There are a host of questions you can ask about each category. If you do not know the answers, make sure you write these information gaps down. Then ask questions during the pitch process, so you can get some strong hints about the suitability of the partnership, short-term and long-term.

Let's look at each category:

CLIENT'S NEEDS

When thinking about the client's current needs, ask yourself the following questions.

What is the urgency or magnitude of the potential client's problem or need?

Clients will be much more willing to talk to you if they have an urgent problem or opportunity and they are aware of it. If on the other hand, they are not conscious of a problem, nor aware of an opportunity, then they will first have to be sold on the problem—before being willing to listen to the solution. There is, however, opportunity here for your organization. If these organizations are unaware of an opportunity, and you are capable of making them see the chance, then there is the possibility that you can pitch for their business without your competitors being involved.

What level of pressure is this client under from competitors in this sector of business?

We find that the more competitive the sector, the more likely the client will be interested in finding better ways to do things. They will be looking for the edge.

Is the client's industry sector expanding or contracting?

Again, if the sector is volatile then opportunities exist for pitching. Change is the catalyst.

What is the degree of dissatisfaction or satisfaction with the client's current supplier?

Unless you have the human resources to squander, or the prize is simply too attractive to give up, don't waste your time pitching to an organization which loves its current supplier. Find an easier target for your services. You could starve before you landed the business.

What is the degree of impact that our product or service will have on the client's business?

Is what you offer of crucial importance to the client decision-maker, or is it only of passing interest? If your product can really add measurable, instant, bottom-line benefits which will dramatically and positively affect the client's business, it will not be too hard to sell. If on the other hand they think of your product once every three years, and then only for seconds, it is going to be a tougher sale.

By thinking about these simple questions, we get an idea about how keen the client is to find a solution.

FINANCIAL ASPECTS

The financial criteria are even more important and they affect both your business and the client's business.

Is there an opportunity cost in us pursuing and/or landing this account?

I've seen many examples where an organization has put all its current accounts at risk by concentrating too much on trying to win one additional account. At the end of the day it may well have won the piece of business, but in doing so it jeopardized or lost the rest of its accounts. The opportunity cost may be that a profitable part of your business will suffer while you risk winning a new account. Your current resources might be more profitably spent elsewhere.

What is the likely profitability of the account to our organization?

Be honest with yourself. I have seen single accounts which have dominated a business to the point where the account runs the supplier. Give close thought to the profit you think you will make. If you have to discount so much that there is nothing left—who wants that sort of client?

What is the cost effectiveness of servicing the business long-term?

Consider the number of team members required to run the business and the possible demands of the client. Think about the client's level of planning and vision, because a client which cannot make decisions about your organization is a client you may not want. Cast your mind into the future. Once you have won the business, how many people and how much of your resources will be needed to support the client?

Can the client pay our bills on the terms we need?

An account which pays cash, or within 30 days, is the only sort of client to have. The client who does not pay at all is the worst, but the client who pays late is not far behind. You do not need them. How many suppliers have won an account only to find that the client doesn't or cannot pay its bills?

BUSINESS POTENTIAL

Think about the business potential of this client.

What is the maximum number of our different products or services that can be sold to this client in the short-term and long-term?

Landing a client is important, but landing a client which can be developed into a *huge* client is better. Is there potential for more of your services and products to be sold to this client?

Is there testimonial benefit?

Will the client name look great on our client list? Will they be willing to let you mention their name when selling to others? A strong client relationship can lead to that client helping you to land another 50 clients.

Is there networking potential between this client and your existing clients?

Synergy between this client and your current customers could lead to benefits for your clients and for you. There may not be immediate profit for you, but you will win in the long-term by strengthening the relationship with other clients.

By studying the business available from each potential client, you can judge how much effort, resources and commitment to put

into the pitch. The possibility of turning the account into something even bigger will affect the way you pitch it.

How hard is this to win?

Now think about how difficult this piece of business may be to
win.

Do we have access to the level of authority or influence which will make the decision?

The old books on selling used to say that you should only sell to
the MAN; that is the person with the Money, the Authority and
the Need. If you have access to, and rapport with, the ultimate
decision-makers, you have an advantage. If you do not have
access, and your competitors do, then you have a real problem.

What does the client think or know about us as a provider of a solution to his current problem?

If your organization image is of such a level that you are well
known to the potential client as being a supplier who can fix a
specific problem, then you have an advantage. If your
organization is not normally associated with the client's industry,
or you are not seen as being a provider of solutions, then you have
a challenge.

What is the ability of this client to make a decision quickly?

Pitching for a piece of business, only to discover that the client
will not commit, is frustrating—if not infuriating. Think about
how the potential client makes decisions. If you are dealing with
the sole decision-maker you should be able to get a fast response,
but if you are working through committees reporting to

committees reporting to management sub-committees, you may be waiting for a long time. And remember, the more people involved in the process of the sale, the more work you will have to do to drive it through. How many of the client's team will be likely to play a role in the decision-making process?

What is the level of skill and/or seniority needed by your team to sell to this client ?

Winning a major account requires skills on your part and on the part of each of your team members. Can you match the level of client expertise? Will your team members be respected as experts in their field? You may have to bolster team talent by hiring a consultant.

What is your existing knowledge of this client's industry, including your previous experience or success in the industry?

The more you know about the client's business, the more likely you will be to win. The investment in educating your team will be less, and you will be more likely to find the best solution. And there is another side. Think about those first few meetings you will have with the client. If you start off speaking the client's language, using the right technical terms, and asking intelligent questions which reflect an inherent knowledge of the industry, you will gain respect. If you begin by asking, 'So, what do you actually do?', then you will lose in the first 30 seconds.

It can often be a subtle, honest mistake that loses the business. The error could be in calling a legal practice an 'organization' instead of a 'firm', referring to advertising account directors as 'salespeople', calling computers 'machines'. Each one proves to clients that you do not understand their business. Find out as much as you can before you start to pitch.

How great is your knowledge of the client's people?

It is not enough to know about the client industry, you also need to know the client decision-maker and their team. The more you know about them, the greater the chance of success. In their minds and hearts lie the keys which will give you access to the business.

Do you have previous successes shared with the client?

If you already have a track record of success, recent or deep in the past, it will help in the pitch. You can utilize that information to help you win.

The degree of difficulty of the sale will affect your team's morale and the effort needed to win. Don't fool yourself into thinking that it will be easy. Make sure you know in advance.

ONGOING RELATIONSHIP

Think about the ongoing relationship you will have with this client.

Do you share similar core values and styles?

Every organization has its own style whether it was deliberately created or just evolved. Rapport will be easier if your organization makes decisions the same way as your client, shares common values, believes in the same sort of vision, has experienced similar growth, decline or experiences.

Can you work well with this client for the period of the contract?

Within your organization may lie values and/or beliefs that might make it difficult to sustain a relationship over a long period. There may be logistical hurdles such as human resources, talent or knowledge. If such barriers are going to be revealed later, thus affecting the long-term relationship, it is best you know now before you decide who to pitch for.

How much pride will you have in running this client?

Some clients make little or no monetary profit for you, but you would not change them for the world. Rogen International was paid virtually nothing for its work on the Sydney 2000 Olympic Bid pitch, but the pride we had in playing our small role made it something we would do again. And the value gained for us in public relations and networking was worth more than many clients generate in two years. However, there are organizations which we would not like to have on our client list, even if we made substantial profit from them.

How faithful is the client likely to be?

I worked with an advertising agency that was fighting to retain a client which it had held for eight years. The tenacity and skill of the agency resulted in a spectacular against-the-odds win. The celebrations were fierce, but within six months the client again called for tenders. Some clients do not hold faithfulness as a core value. They change suppliers, not for valid reasons, but because 'it might be interesting to find out what else is available'. Check out the client track record regarding supplier longevity.

TIMING

Finally, give some consideration to the timing aspects of the pitch.

Is the client ready to act now?

Make sure the client is able and willing to consider an approach. Offer bread to a starving person, not to someone who has just eaten.

Do you know what is influencing the timing of a decision?

What will govern how quickly this organization will decide to seek a new supplier? Is it the annual budget period? Is there a new marketing director, pressure from overseas parent organizations, a new product release?

Can you alter the client's perception of urgency?

Perhaps you can persuade the client that there is a need to act now. If you could, what would be the trigger?

Can you afford to wait?

Can you afford to wait for the business if it is not available right now, for whatever reason and, if so, for how long? Perhaps you can make some minor moves now which will stand your organization in good stead when the business does finally become available.

Is the client worth waiting for?

There will be times when your business is such that you can only have one major client in each industry sector to avoid a conflict of interests. If that is the case, and this client is not available now, is another organization a better option, or should you wait?

SUMMARY

By applying these few questions before and during the process, you become capable of making an informed judgment about how much you want to win the business. Many cannot be answered without talking to the client, so the information will be gathered as the process continues. But even by applying what you do know or have read about a client, you will end up with a prioritized list.

You may want to start pitching for some clients tomorrow, others may constitute business that you would love to have, but they will not be available for some time. The first sort is urgent business and these are the clients you want right now!

The second category is equally important, but a strategy can be developed over a longer period. Assign a person or team to monitor the long-term potential client. Keep a file filled with clippings, reports, press releases and snippets of information. Make sure your team begins to build rapport, gains access to decision-makers and key influencers within the organization, keeps your organization name in front of them, knows the industry, supplies the client with faxes and clippings from overseas and local sources—starts to influence.

If the client passes the process with flying colours and you still believe it is an account that you can win, and desperately *want* to win, then you can begin the pitch.

Chapter 8

Getting on
the Pitch list
and Selecting
your Team

THERE ARE MANY BOOKS written by others on how to promote yourself and your organization—how to cold call and how to get invited to pitch. So I'm not going to spend a lot of time on the subject. Suffice to say that if you're not known by the prospect you will never be invited to pitch. So get known—it only takes hard work.

✦ Promote yourself with publicity, direct mail and advertising.

✦ Be seen where your prospects are seen—at conferences, golf days and industry meetings.

✦ Ring the prospect and introduce yourself.

✦ Write the prospect a letter.

✦ Read the industry papers and cut out items which you think will interest prospective clients. Fax these items to the client at 8 am to show them you care. Personalize every communication so they feel they know you.

✦ Send them a note of congratulations when you read about their achievements.

✦ Ask if you can present your credentials.

✦ Invite them to a function at your head office.

✦ Add value to their organization without asking for anything in return—an industry survey, a fascinating article from an overseas paper which they may not have seen.

✦ Attack their organization at several entry points, using different people and different strategies.

Lo and behold, you've started to build rapport, and sooner or later the time will be right for you to ask if you can pitch for their business.

More often than not, they will ask you, along with others. The telephone call will come and you will find yourself on a pitch list.

Now the pitch is on and it's time to get serious! Every single thing that you do from now on can affect the result. So take care.

Unfortunately a lot of business is lost in the very first meeting. Too often the desire to rush out and meet a prospective client leads to that client's business going elsewhere. It's ironic that the very enthusiasm so indispensable in winning the account will often lose it during the first meeting.

When that enquiry comes in from a potential client, the tendency is to rush out and meet them, to find out more about what they want. But the danger is that by going in unprepared, you will say the wrong thing, prove that you do not understand their business and come away without key information you need.

TIP

Get into an organization at all levels.

If you have sales representatives, then have them network with the prospect's representatives. Get your chairman to network with theirs, your marketing director to meet theirs. Get into the client's business at all levels.

TIP

Budget time for planning.

When the big call comes in, make sure you allow a few days before that initial meeting. Give yourself time to study the client

continued...

situation, so you will appear perceptive on first impression.

The first meeting needs planning too.

In the time you have, find out everything you can about the client's industry, the organization and the people that you are going to see. By going in talking their language and avoiding pitfalls, you will be on the way to winning the account. You'll still be there primarily to listen, but your probing will be intelligent and perceptive.

SELECTING YOUR PITCH TEAM

Your pitch team should combine technical expertise with flair—sound thinking with wild ideas—attention to detail with vision.

Appoint a *pitch team leader*. This person will be responsible for coordinating and leading the pitch. Everyone will report to the team leader and they will be responsible for calling meetings and directing the effort.

Team leaders need two main abilities. They must be able to motivate and they must be able to organize.

Their motivation will drive the team, showing the way, getting people excited, showing that a win is possible, playing down disappointment, being innovative.

Their coordinating strength will ensure that everything is on target and on time, that each player has the help they need, that each facet of the pitch is fitting into the overall plan.

The team leader is the key driver on the road to success. Without a leader the pitch is destined to fail.

Someone needs to be the *pitch coordinator*, setting up the meetings when the team leader requests, collecting data, researching, following through, arranging the rooms and equipment. You may need outside consultants with expertise in areas of the prospect's business or that industry.

TIP

Select a blend of styles.

The well-rounded pitch team has some analytical, process-driven members, some amiable types with strong people values, some very direct, business-driven styles and finally some expressive, creative members. This blend will improve your brainstorming outcomes and will give you a better chance to match personalities with the client team.

You will need strong communication skills for the times when you meet the client's executives: a writer for the final document and presentation skills for the pitch. You may need your advertising agency to produce materials quickly and creatively. You may need your public relations company to coordinate some publicity during the pitch.

TIP

Pitches take time.

Invest the time to do a pitch well, and be aware that the investment can be a big one. If the pitch is on, clear your slate of other projects and make sure that your team members have time to spare as well.

BUILDING THE WAR ROOM

Assemble your team and start the planning by building yourself a 'war room'.

The 'war room' will be the focal point within your organization, for the team handling the pitch—a place where the latest information is available. Ideally, it should be a small room where team members can brainstorm. Its walls should be filled with information on flipchart paper tacked to pin boards. The information on the walls of the room should evolve as the pitch process continues, so anyone on the team can bring themselves up to date with what is happening in the pitch.

The war room should have a table and chairs, coffee, flipcharts and coloured markers. It can be kept locked to protect the confidentiality of the pitch.

Separate charts on the wall will cover specific subjects. Put a bold heading on each chart and fill it with information as it becomes available. You will probably already have some data, but you will add more as you gather and check. There should be one chart for each subject.

TIP

> Appoint a Flipchart Writer.
>
> Make sure that you have one team member who is capable of quickly drawing legible flipcharts. Trying to decipher scribble is not conducive to sound planning.

CHART ONE: OUR COMPANY (STRENGTHS AND WEAKNESSES)

Objective: To enable you to place emphasis on your strengths during the pitch, and to help focus on what you need to add or downplay to cover your weaknesses.

Content: Create two columns. In the first write up the *strengths* of your organization *as seen by the prospect* and then candidly list the *weaknesses.* The relevant strengths and weaknesses are only those which affect this pitch. You will have started this sort of thinking earlier when you sat down to decide what your organization had to offer in general. Now you need to tailor it for this specific prospect and this piece of business. If the client mentions another strength or weakness in a meeting, add it to the chart. To find your weaknesses, think what your competitors could be saying about you.

CHART TWO: COMPETITORS (STRENGTHS AND WEAKNESSES)

Objectives: To understand the 'enemy' and to provide opportunities for you to highlight their weaknesses and down play their strengths. These key charts, in combination with your own strengths and weaknesses chart, will show you where the opportunity lies and where the threats could occur.

Content: The same as for your strengths and weaknesses chart, but this time do one chart for each supplier pitching against you for the business. List their strengths and weaknesses, again from the point of view of the client. Add to these charts as you find out information in the days or weeks leading up to the final presentation.

CHART THREE: THE PITCH CRITICAL PATH

Objectives: To understand how much time you have to prepare, and to coordinate each team member's actions into a master plan.

Content: Chart a critical path leading up to the presentation, and a week beyond that day. List actions planned for each day. Put in each strategy meeting, each rehearsal, each client meeting, deadlines for the written proposal, for each department's input.

The final weeks should be listed day by day to allow for the inevitable last minute rush. A sound critical path enables each team member to work on their own, knowing that at certain times they need to meet, and at other times they will be expected to produce information, ideas and products.

CHART FOUR: CLIENT PERSONNEL

Objective: To focus on each individual in the final selection panel and to understand their needs, values and role.

Content: Do one chart for each person on the client panel, whether or not they are decision-makers. Include the following details:

✦   name;

✦   title;

✦   a curriculum vitae if available;

✦   anything which may have been published about them;

✦   their perceived role in the decision;

✦   their perceived attitude to your organization;

✦ their key needs; and

✦ the issues which they most want targeted.

As your team members get to meet each person, listen for buzz words they use and key issues which they raise—find out what turns them on. Come back to the war room and write them on the chart.

What will each person say if, two weeks after you are appointed, a colleague asks, 'Why did you appoint them?' How will this person rationalize the decision? Put it all on the charts.

Chart Five: publicity board

Objective: To keep up to date with what is happening in the marketplace. Large account pitches tend to create publicity in and beyond the trade media.

Content: Cut out all clippings from trade journals and newspapers and stick them to the chart. Hire a clipping service on the client's industry during the pitch and put all relevant clippings up on the chart. In this way you will all be up to date with terminology and issues affecting the industry and the client. During the meetings before the pitch and during the final presentation your team will be using terminology which shows you understand the client's business.

Chart Six: industry rumours

Objective: To be aware of industry murmurs and talk. If others are hearing what you are hearing it could affect their strategy. Sometimes the rumours are even right!

Content: Have a chart on which you can write any rumours that you pick up during the pitch. Most will be fallacious, but some may lead to facts. You will hear them from your own suppliers, from the trade, from friends. Don't discount any, but trust few. And remember, you can start rumours too, if it suits your goals.

CHART SEVEN: OUR PITCH TEAM

Objective: To clearly define the roles of your pitch team members so there is no misunderstanding at any time, and so team members seeking information know who to approach.

Content: List your pitch team, and each person's role in the process, in the presentation itself and in running the account when it is acquired. If they are specifically looking after certain aspects of the information gathering, then note that too.

CHART EIGHT: OUR PRESENTATION STRUCTURE

Objective: To start the team focusing on the content of the presentation, and who will be saying what.

Content: Draw up a rough structure for the presentation itself. When you have more information you can put up who will speak first, second, third and so on, the key points they will make, how long each segment will take. In Chapter 15 I will give you a team presentation structure.

CHART NINE: KEY TAKE-OUTS

Objective: To focus on the one, two or three things that the client will remember after the pitch.

Content: When you know them, write up the key take-outs which the client will walk away with after your presentation. What do you want them to remember about your pitch? Don't think up six key take-outs. Nobody ever remembers more than three.

CHART TEN: BRAINSTORMING

Objective: To capture every crazy, creative idea before it is forgotten.

Content: Create a chart for crazy ideas, left-field thoughts that might lead to something exciting. Have everyone write them up as they come to mind. Go back to them occasionally and check to see if they might work.

CHART ELEVEN: THE THEME

Objective: To develop a theme for the presentation. The best presentations have a theme, a memorable thread which runs from beginning to end. The theme might be 'partnership' or 'together into the next century' or 'it's war!'. Having a theme rather than a technical subject shows flair and makes the pitch more entertaining.

Content: Start to collect ideas for this theme. Write them up. You can accept or reject them later.

CHART TWELVE: THE POWER MAP

Objective: To plot the impact that each person involved will have in making the decision. Understanding this will keep you focused on the right people and the right issues. This chart often requires the most thought.

Content: Make a map which reflects the power of individuals within the client's organization. It is a vital part of your strategy and I have covered it in Chapter 9.

By this stage your war room walls are filled with mostly blank sheets of paper. But already your team can focus on the real information required. From now on every available piece of useful information is put onto the charts. Information gaps are found and as quickly as possible filled.

The team meets in the war room at specific times to add information, change it and modify the strategy as necessary. If it is impossible to meet as a team, individual team members can open the room and find the information they need, or add or modify data on the appropriate chart.

The war room is the best room in the building for individuals to sit and think because its walls display the latest information about the pitch. The room's walls evolve as the pitch continues.

You now have a focus for the process, but you still need to go out and gather information.

Chapter 9

Who are we pitching to?

Peter Rogen once told me: 'You can't sell anything...unless you have someone to sell it to. You can't tell a story, unless you have someone who will listen to it. How can you be convincing, without anyone to convince?'

You win or lose pitches on sound listener analysis, because it doesn't matter how good your strategy, how brilliant your creative concept, how exciting your product—unless you can convince the people in the room, you can throw it into the trash can. If ideas aren't sold well, they're not sold at all.

Each person involved in the client's decision-making process has their own conscious or subconscious needs and their personal motivations for appointing one or another supplier.

Why do people buy a pair of Reeboks? How much of that decision is emotional? Would Moet et Chandon champagne sell as well if it were not expensive? Why does a middle-aged man buy a massively powerful motor cruiser? Why buy a Ferrari when speed limits are such that you never get out of second gear?

Emotional decision-making is a fact of life and, believe it or not, the size of the decision doesn't necessarily change anything.

When a pitch is in progress, we first need to find, then monitor, the relative importance of rational (and technical) needs and motivators, against those needs which are emotional, political or cultural.

UNDERSTANDING RATIONAL NEEDS

The client will most easily discuss their rational and technical needs. These will dominate the written brief, for example:

✦ the price must be the lowest, within budget;

✦ the solution will solve the client's problem or deliver the most tangible benefits;

✦ the solution should fit the client's overall vision;

✦ the timing must be right;

✦ delivery must be right;

✦ the quality must be right;

✦ it is technically excellent; and so on.

The rational and technical parts of the brief are the 'tick the box' issues. Sydney had hundreds of technical boxes to be ticked to prove itself capable of staging the 2000 Olympics. And in its final presentation we ticked them all.

UNDERSTANDING EMOTION

The technical arguments that you put in your pitch give the decision-makers the evidence they need to rationalise their emotional decisions. But in their hearts lie the emotional motivations. I've seen pitches won using emotional strategies of all kinds, for example:

✦ ego (strategy for an advertising agency: 'Put the client's photo in the advertisements!');

✦ ambition (strategy: 'This appointment is going to do wonders for your career!');

+ fear (strategy: 'You can't risk changing suppliers now!');

+ trust (strategy: 'Our track record shows our reliability.');

+ security (strategy: 'You'll be in very good hands.');

+ familiarity (strategy: 'We're like you, we understand what you need.');

+ greed (strategy: 'This solution will make you rich!').

These factors—rational and emotional—impact on every sale ever made. What are the rational reasons for a person buying a Rolls Royce motor car? An owner will be the first to tell you—resale value, quality, good engineering, size and so on.

But what are the emotional reasons? They might not be as willing to share those with a stranger. Perhaps Rolls Royce ownership proves that the owner has arrived at the top of the tree? Perhaps there is ego involved, or pride, or ambition—all needs which can be satisfied by a purchase.

But while the emotional needs can outweigh the rational two to one, they have to be treated with circumspection. A Rolls Royce salesperson would do well *not* to greet a prospective buyer by saying, 'Ah! I see that you have come from a blue-collar background and you want to prove that you've finally achieved a position in life'.

UNDERSTANDING POLITICS

Politics impinge on most decisions these days. Current values limit our decision making or force us to go in one direction rather than another. This final category of need is also critical in understanding what motivates someone to buy your organization's services.

By seeking the motivators for each of the people in the organization we will gain an understanding of the issues in the minds and hearts of each person in the decision-making process.

The least this thinking can achieve is a list of questions which can be asked to plug in the gaps in our knowledge—gaps currently filled by assumptions. While the information is being gathered and collated, and discussed and shared, other things can be running concurrently. The team will be finding the solution to the client's stated problem and gathering persuasive information which can be used later. But while this essential work is happening, others will be searching for the edge, for the special information that might point to a winning tactic. The answer lies in the audience, provided you are prepared to dig for it.

Audience research can be the most time-consuming part of pitch preparation, but it is time and money well spent. With this basic building block in place, the rest of your preparation will be on track. Get audience analysis wrong, however, and it doesn't matter how much evidence you may have collected or how much you have spent creating your visual aids.

If you don't agree, then try to sell your services to an audience of total strangers, each of whom may or may not know anything about your organization, may or may not care anything about it, may be different from the others in style, race, age, knowledge and temperament. You don't know the audience members at all, how they make decisions or even if they are capable of making decisions. They may be seething with anger over something that has happened to them recently; they may have preconceptions about you or your organization—but you do not know any of this.

That frightening scenario is faced every day by poorly prepared presenters. I've seen the heads of major service organizations walk into a boardroom to pitch for millions of dollars worth of business—without knowing who they will face on the other side of the door. Common sense says that if someone has been asked to be in the audience, they must have some influence on the decision, however slight.

Now imagine another scenario—convincing an audience of 10 business colleagues, each of whom the presenter has worked with for five years, each of whom is a social friend. The presenter has a deep knowledge of each listener's style, their background, likes and dislikes, values, preference in visual aids, ability to take in technical data and so on.

Which would you rather face? The second is an ideal situation and the first scenario is a lottery, i.e. the odds are no better. In the end the objective of your pitch is to have decision-makers and their key influencers react positively to do something—buy your offer, be persuaded. Without them there is no pitch.

The following three categories of potential clients will decide whether you win or not:

1. The decision-maker.

    This person has the power and the position to say yes or no. Despite that, decision-makers most often seek the counsel of others before making a major choice.

2. The key influencer.

    Financial controllers, marketing directors, partners, human resource managers, category managers—if these people are not decision-makers themselves, these are the people to whom the decision-maker usually turns for advice. Their judgment can make or break a pitch.

3. The influencer.

    Anyone else who is part of the pitch or has the ability to influence the decision is an influencer, and should be included in your strategy.

Each has a role to play in making the decision. As a rule, if someone is in the room as part of your audience, they are at least an influencer. If it is a close decision, their vote could tip you over the top. Ignore any one of them at your peril. The challenge is to find the relative importance of each person in the decision-making process, with a view to applying appropriate influence on each.

A few years ago it was often as simple as looking for the MAN— the person with the Money, the Authority and the Need. One person controlled the decision and your level of understanding of that person would govern your success. But management has been changing—major decisions involving millions of dollars tend to demand consensus decision-making.

A more sophisticated approach is required when selling into large organizations or selling to committees. It is necessary to ascertain correctly the power within an organization as it relates specifically to having your organization appointed.

Power is the 'ability to do or act'. (In the case of your situation, power is the ability to approve the appointment of your organization as supplier.)

Interestingly enough, power is only visible when change is occurring; that is, when something is happening, when people are being asked to do things, when a decision is being made which will have an effect, however small, on the organization. When this situation occurs, power can be seen in play. When nothing is changing, real power sinks below the line of visibility and is harder to find, although the trappings of power still remain. People can claim to have it, and can even appear to have it, but the proof will be found when something is changing.

The power you are interested in is the power affecting your appointment as a supplier.

Consider individuals in the political structure of an organization, from two points of view:

1. The degree of authority, that is, the right to make things happen.

2. The degree of influence, that is, the effect they have on others.

Any organization has individuals with different amounts of these two key ingredients: authority and influence. But having one or the other does not necessarily create power.

DECISION-MAKERS

There are, however, those with both the authority and the influence. They have the right to enforce change and they have an effect on others. They are the decision-makers. They are the power. There are those with authority but without the influence to get others to act—for instance, the CEO who sends out memos but nothing happens—they are the rubber stampers. You can be less worried about them in the pitch, provided they are absolute 'rubber stampers'. But experience shows that such people rarely exist in such a homogeneous form.

KEY INFLUENCERS

There are those with influence but no authority. They can persuade and cajole and motivate others to follow. Their influence can be so strong in some cases that the person with authority might bow to the influencer, even though the influencer does not have the right to force the change. They are influencers or key influencers depending on the effect they can have on the decision-makers.

COLLECTORS

There are also those with neither authority nor influence. They tend to simply collect information and act as a conduit to those with either influence or power, or both. They are the collectors. They can help you or hinder you depending on the level of rapport or respect you share.

And there are those, crazy as it seems, who will be on the panel but who will play no role at all. They are the socials. I seldom see a case where someone is asked to be on the panel, yet has absolutely no influence on the panel's decision; but politics allow it to happen, and both small and large organizations have politics.

The decision to buy what you are selling will occur due the interaction of the above people.

THE POWER MAP

Draw the power map on the war room wall, starting with the person with whom you had first contact in the organization.

Fill out all the boxes of the players involved and attribute to them a title from the list above. It might look something like the diagram on the following page.

Nominate a percentage amount for each person in the decision-making process. Modify it as you learn more. The power map helps you and your team to understand who is important and who is not, and their relative influence on the decision.

Sometimes the CEO might be the decision-maker. At other times it might be the product manager. Make sure you get it right. The decision-maker is not always obvious. Be wary of the client contact who tells you that he or she is the sole decision-maker— it is not always the truth. Ego gets in the way of accuracy.

Now that you have a power map showing the various players in the organization, the task is to harness each of these decision-makers or influencers to obtain the collective or individual decision to approve your appointment.

The power map will probably evolve as you move into the process. That's to be encouraged.

Understanding the influence of each person in the decision-making process is one component of the solution. Understanding what motivates them is the second part. Without a deep knowledge of the decision-makers and key influencers, you may

POWER MAP

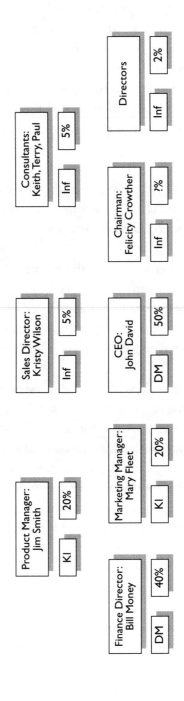

Product Manager: Jim Smith — KI 20%	Sales Director: Kristy Wilson — Inf 5%	Consultants: Keith, Terry, Paul — Inf 5%	
Marketing Manager: Mary Fleet — KI 20%			Directors — Inf 2%
Finance Director: Bill Money — DM 40%	CEO: John David — DM 50%	Chairman: Felicity Crowther — Inf ?%	

KEY: Key influencer: KI; Influencer: Inf; Decision-maker: DM or may not find out what influences them. You may or may not be able to select the appropriate amount of the right kind of evidence needed to convince them. You may or may not be able to answer the questions they ask. What you need is information—about their industry, their sector, their organization and them—because information is the driver of strategy.

Lack of data about the audience members and the situation surrounding the pitch will force you to make assumptions. Then, on the shifting base of those assumptions, you tend to add more, making more assumptions based on assumptions based on assumptions, then...

The danger was known in the Middle Ages. English philosopher William of Ockham (1280-1349) said, 'No more things shall be presumed to exist than are absolutely necessary'. More new business pitches are lost because they were based on assumptions (which later proved wrong) than for any other reason.

Examples are everywhere: an Australian fast-food group, seeking an advertising agency to run its seven million dollar account, approached several Australian agencies, including the local branch of the agency which handled its advertising in the USA. The Australian advertising agency logically assumed that the potential client had invited them to pitch because of their US links. They made a strong point of including a video of their US agency talking positively about them. That was a wrong assumption. The fast-food chain not only did not want the US agency involved, they considered it presumptuous to think that the US was better at marketing than Australia. The pitch was lost.

Avoid assumptions. Replace them with facts gained by talking to the client, or those who know the client.

Many would argue that sometimes it is not possible to find out much about an audience. The truth is that there is little that cannot be found out if you know the right questions to ask, and the right places to look for answers.

The objective of audience analysis is to get to a point where you are talking to people whom you understand and who understand you. Importantly, they need also to realize that you understand their business, because that is the sort of supplier they want. They certainly do not want to have to waste time educating you.

The closer you can get to having a comprehensive understanding of the audience, their problems and their opportunities, the less chance there will be of putting your foot in it, or of failing to interest the listeners.

In your first meeting as a pitch team discuss and answer these questions: 'Who do we need to see?' and 'What do we need to ask them?'

Chapter 10

The Rogen Questionnaire

WE FIRST USED the Rogen International Questionnaire when helping the advertising agency Weekes, Morris, Osborn win the $40 million Qantas Airways advertising account. Its use demonstrated professionalism and a methodical, analytical approach which appealed to the decision-makers and key influencers at Qantas and focused an excellent agency pitch team. You simply ask all the decision-makers and key influencers the same 10 or 20 questions. It's a way to cross-check with great accuracy the answers that the main players give to the same issues. It shows up mismatches in values and understanding and points the way to the real questions which need answering. And it's so easy!

Design a questionnaire for each person on the client team who can supply the sort of information which might put an end to an assumption. Your pitch team should think very carefully about the questions they want to ask. Some of those that you will interview will need questions specific to them. But ideally the same questions should be asked of all.

Sound questions, based on preparation and insightful thinking, project a favourable image of competence and professionalism. Preparation of these questions is critical to successful selling.

The questions you ask should lead to a deeper level of information, so in probing each issue you need to include open-ended questions. For example:

◆ What thoughts or ideas have you about...?
   What feelings...?
   What opinions...?
   What reasons...?

Why...?

What methods or ways...?

How...?

Could you tell me about...?

Could you give me a picture of...?

Could you explain...?

◆ Compare/outline/review/trace...?

Could you describe...?

The subject matter of your probing will depend on what you *really* want to know that was not included in the initial brief. So, depending on your industry, you could probe the client's attitude to the following:

◆ the current supplier;

◆ the way the organization currently feels about the supplier sector;

◆ what they like about and what could be improved about the current relationship;

◆ key issues contained in the brief about which you need more information; and

◆ weighting of issues described in the brief, for example, 'how important do you feel X is in relation to Y?';

Here are some more key general questions to have answered, either by the client or from other areas which I will discuss later:

Who are the final decision-makers?

Some situations will have one decision-maker who will be so dominant that it really only matters that you convince them. The opinion of the others can almost be discounted. But this is less often the case. In fact I would go so far as to say that if there are other people invited to sit in on the final pitch, then there is little or no chance that the decision has already been made by one person. The exception would be if politics have overcome ethics, but it is more likely in that environment that the decision-maker is seeking advice from colleagues. That makes the colleagues an important part of the decision-making process.

Are there people who are not final decision-makers but are key influencers?

It is more likely that any major decision situation will have more than one decision-maker and several key influencers, that is, people who may not make the decision but will certainly be consulted by the decision-maker. Occasionally you may have an audience in which everybody has one equal vote—a situation which actually seems to be increasing as a means of selecting service companies and consultancies.

What is their decision-making pattern?

This is a great area to probe. How will the decision actually be made? The answers will give you an insight into the organization itself and the politics involved. Ask how the client makes decisions on similar issues—quickly, slowly, by consensus, using consultants, using head office?

How much money are they prepared to spend?

This is an interesting area to investigate, and can lead to some valuable insights. It's always wise to check the actual amount the account is worth to the client as opposed to that which the client claims is available. I recall a $20 million dollar advertising account which was won by one of my advertising agency clients. The win was celebrated within the agency with a party and champagne. Unfortunately, the client then spent less than $100,000 over the next year, spread over several divisions. So much for $20 million. Probe the financial area closely. The work which you did earlier will have shown information gaps which you can now fill.

How much do they know?

This is another key area to explore with the client. What's the current level of knowledge held by the client—not just about your organization, but about their own business, their own market, the issues that face them, marketing in general? By probing carefully you will get a clear understanding of the level of knowledge held by the client. You need to find out where the current understanding lies, then you will see what education may be required before it becomes obvious that your solution is the best one.

What do they want?

The difference between what they actually need, and what they believe they *want,* can be like chalk and cheese. But often the desires of the client need to be addressed first before the needs can be satisfied. What are the benefits they desire from a relationship with your organization? What is on their wish-list? In an ideal world what would they really love to have? Explore this area to check for misconceptions about your organization's role.

What do they need?

Probe the technical and rational needs and, importantly, what elements are essential from the client's point of view. If you cannot supply these, it is better that you know now, not later.

In terms of content and presentation style, what does your client expect to see and hear in your final presentation?

This should be checked out early in the process, before you start planning the event itself. What are they used to in presentations and proposals? Should you give them what they have asked the other suppliers to present, or can you go further? How long have you got to present? Are questions separate to that? Where is the presentation to be held? Who will be there? Formal or informal?

Ask if there are areas which you should *not* cover in your presentation. Find out why.

The way you present will affect their perception of your organization but, if they specifically ask that you do not present in a certain way, then you need to think carefully about that request. Advertising agencies, for example, are often asked to present only strategy, without creative execution. But usually any agency responding to that brief will go beyond the strategy to show examples of how the creative execution might look. The reason is that creativity sells and strategy does not. Creativity is the sizzle of the steak, strategy the raw meat itself. However, I know of at least one agency that defied the client's ruling about not including creative execution. And they lost for that reason.

How much and what kind of technical information is being sought by the decision-makers?

This area opens up a world of opportunities. The answers will give you hints as to whether these people are rational, analytical decision-makers or whether they are more impressed by motivation and vision. Analytical people require information to be presented in a way which shows logic and progression, with amply demonstrated background and knowledge. The expressive audience may want to be excited by a vision and shown the light at the end of the tunnel. Understanding how the client deals with facts and figures can help you decide how you will present technical data later, if at all.

What 'turns them on'?

What motivates these people? What would be the most exciting thing you could say to these decision-makers? Find out if the client is impressed by achieving goals or by seeing plans come to fruition, by praise or by results? Ask about previous achievements the organization has made—see if they get excited and remember what it was that inspired them.

What factors might influence the decision?

Are there extraneous factors which will affect how the client moves on this decision? For example, is there something extra that you could offer, as part of your solution, that might influence a yes vote?

Ask yourself how far you can go outside the brief to provide a solution.

Probe this whole area to see if the client is conservative or dynamic. How 'outlandish' can your solution be? Will a bold solution score points or be seen as too wild? This area of probing will help you check the client's position on the continuum which runs between conservative and dynamic. The knowledge will be of benefit to you later.

I tell the story of a team of architects who flew to another State to pitch for a piece of business. They were young and brash and dressed in the latest fashion. They walked into the boardroom and found themselves facing a panel of decision-makers, all wearing brown business suits. The managing partner in the architecture firm told me later: 'I knew we were in trouble when I saw the hat-rack outside the boardroom door. It had six brown hats on it. Everything we did clashed with their conservatism.'

Probe what attitudes the client has towards you and your company.

Is it how you want to be perceived? Can you affect that perception? You may have to rebuild some fences caused by past actions or interpretation of those actions or, on a positive note, you may find things that you have done which the client liked and admired. You can stress them later in your pitch.

What is their work background, social background and educational level?

This is very personal information, but if you start probing their business background, and things are going well, you can often keep going into their personal life. If rapport is increasing, then keep probing. There are values hidden in these areas; values which will help you position your benefits for maximum impact.

What are they especially proud of or loyal to?

What do they most like about what they do? Again there are important values which lie in these areas. They may have strong organization core values. They may be proud of their past achievements. They may be fiercely loyal to their organization and/or its leader. That knowledge is priceless to you.

Whose opinion do they respect?

Probe how they feel about industry leaders; perhaps, if you have the opportunity, even your country's leaders. How do they feel about their opposition companies, about other suppliers? Tread carefully but, if you have rapport, you can often get answers which will help you set tone and mood later—and avoid saying things which are better left unsaid.

When you have brainstormed a list of 10 or 20 questions which you feel will deliver the greatest value to you in your search for the real needs of the organization, have them typed up with one question per page, leaving space beneath to write the interviewee's replies. Bind the questions into a folder and put the name of each individual being interviewed on the front cover. This shows that person that they are important and that you want their personal opinion.

Now start interviewing.

Chapter 11

Rapport Building and Probing

ALWAYS THINK CAREFULLY about which members of your team are best suited in style to interview key people on the client side. You may prefer to send two members of your team to each interview, making sure that each has a different business style. One might be a very direct person, the other analytical; or one might be creative and the other direct. Once you get into the meeting and are better able to ascertain the style of the client, one of your team members will play a more dominant role to increase rapport and thus get the questions answered.

Because the interview component of the pitch process is often where you win or lose, it must be handled by skilled communicators, who know how to build rapport.

Don't underestimate the need for compatibility. The quality of the answers depends on the level of rapport which exists at the time the questions are asked. Put simplistically, if they don't either like you, look up to you or respect you as a professional, they are not going to tell you what you want to know.

A skilled communicator is a skilled listener. At Rogen International we call it 'Listening someone into a sale' as opposed to 'Talking someone into a sale'.

At times it will be better to send your best communicator alone. Don't send someone who is a poor one-on-one communicator, who finds it hard to establish rapport and to probe. Whoever you send, be very conscious of the fact that the choice must not be made lightly. You may not be pitching formally at this stage, but you are still pitching. If your interviewer clashes with the decision-maker at this stage, you will have a lot of ground to make up even to get back to where you began.

Given the crucial nature of these initial encounters, you should give each one the planning it deserves.

Remember that your focus should always be one-on-one. When you present to the client later in the pitch process you want to give each individual in the audience exactly what they need from your team. And to discover those needs, you have to find out their individual feelings. Only someone with effective one-on-one communication skills can do this job successfully.

Stage-manage every meeting. The purpose of each interview session is fourfold:

1. to build rapport;

2. to get real answers to the real issues;

3. to show the person that you understand their business; and

4. to find personal agenda.

As a pitch team, plan the appropriate tone, mood, objective and take-outs for every person being interviewed. Do you want to be seen as informal and friendly, or formal and 'MBA'? What do you want the interviewee to do as a result of the meeting? What do you want the client to think about you and your organization?

If the meeting is with the client's financial director, you may want to show an understanding of the need to contain costs. If it is with the sales manager, the take-out may be that of boosting sales. If with the marketing manager, the outcome may be that you prove you understand their customers. Remember that each person interviewed has different needs and must be treated differently. If you want to be perceived as being business-like and buttoned-up, think about sending an agenda in advance.

Make sure that your team interviews every single person who will be at the pitch more than once, and ideally several times. Every meeting is a pitch in its own right. You can win or lose the business every time you meet. Here are some guidelines for communicating in a lead-up meeting.

RAPPORT—THE CORNERSTONE OF THE PITCH

How many times have you dealt with a salesperson you dislike and do not respect? How many times have you shared important information with that person? The answer is seldom or never. If you do not like someone, or look up to them, or respect them, you will be reluctant to tell them anything of importance.

However, if you feel they share much in common with you, or if you respect them for their success, or respect them for being a professional in their area of business, then you are more likely to talk to them openly and honestly.

This is why rapport is essential in any interview. Without it the answers will be less valuable. Rapport starts with the first communication, and communication starts when they first talk to you or see you.

Monitor rapport very closely during the meeting process. If you feel it failing, back off. On the other hand, look for winning signals. Ask the client for a favour; if it is done willingly, you have a degree of rapport.

TIP

Don't talk business—talk feelings.

There is more power in talking about how you feel about things than in talking about the business aspects of an issue. And it is a winning signal when a potential client begins to talk about their feelings rather than limiting the conversation to the rational side of the situation. Seek to move the conversation to feelings, but be careful. Moving too soon, or at all, may damage rapport.

A winning signal is when the person volunteers something that did not have to be given, ranging from openness, to giving out confidential information or intimating the politics of the organization. If the client does something for you, you are doing very well. For example, they may give you extra information, or agree to let you pitch first, or last, or agree to another meeting, or share a confidence.

Rapport should be building each time you meet.

PROBING WITH PURPOSE

A real estate friend once told me that the first question he ever asked of a client looking to buy a house was, 'What don't you like about your current home?' I love that probe. It cuts right through the fog and forces the interviewee to think deeply about the subject. Use the same technique in your interviews. Check attitudes to the current supplier. What went wrong? What didn't they like about their current supplier? In there often lies the clue to your strategy.

There is a second question that I also love. It's called a focus probe: 'If there is one thing you would like to improve over your current service, what would that be?' That's a powerful tool.

Both these questions are examples of the sort of probing that will get you 'real' answers—rather than 'right' answers. Probing is the art of acquiring information while increasing rapport. At the start of the pitch you and your team have a thousand questions and no answers. It's logical that the best people to give you the answers are those to whom you will be presenting. They will make the decision, so what they say is gold.

So see them more often that your competitors. It's not widely practised, but a pitch team should spend more time interviewing than it ever spends writing the pitch or rehearsing.

The interviews themselves should never be interrogations. They should be relaxed, comfortable talks with the client, sharing information, listening and asking all at the same time. A good communicator will listen to the other person, without the threat of action. They do not listen simply to refute or argue, but because it is interesting. Listening is one of the most valuable pitching skills you can have. It is not something done to fill the gaps between passages of your speech. It is more valuable than words, so your words should aid your listening. Learn to pose questions and listen actively.

Use close-ended and open-ended questions combined with personal comments. Close-ended questions such as: Who? When? Where? How much/long/many? Either/or? Which? Yes or no? These can be combined with open-ended questions to get longer answers, and to start learning thoughts and feelings in greater depth. What thoughts/ideas have you about...? What feelings? What opinions? What reasons? Why? What methods/ways? How? Could you tell me about...? Could you give me a picture of...? Could you explain...? Could you compare/outline/review/ trace? Could you describe?

Remember, effective listening will help put an end to assumptions. And making assumptions is the kiss of death in new business pitching.

Here are five points to keep in mind:

1. Prepare key questions ahead of time, using your questionnaire.

2. Plan the timing of your questions. It may not be appropriate to ask some sensitive questions on the first meeting. Plan to ask them later, once you have a degree of rapport.

3. Be alert to situations that require unplanned questions, such as if you see the prospect looking puzzled or bewildered or confused.

4. Have a specific purpose in mind for each question you ask.

5. Ask questions that can lead to something you sell. Don't widen the conversation until you are wasting your time and the client's time.

The obvious outcomes you seek from the probing process include establishing rapport with the client, gaining an insight into the business, helping the client to gain a new insight into the business, changing the way things have been looked at, showing you understand the client and proving can help.

Your objective is to find the values that guide them in making decisions. What are the values they have picked up from life? What values are currently imposed on them by their role, their organization, their culture, their peers, their personal situation? If you do it well, you will end up enjoying the process and liking each other more than you did at the start. But get it wrong and you can destroy rapport entirely. There is a difference between probing and prying!

Communicate with everyone who will be involved in the process, even if they will not all be present for the pitch itself. Actively listen until you understand them and they you, and until rapport exists.

Study each person until you know their emotional and rational motivators, until you understand the politics which drives them and their relationship with the others in the pitch. Explore others who have dealt with the client. Question them all.

If you interview well, you are already helping to win the business. You are building rapport. You are being appreciated. You are seeking knowledge which you can use later. You are showing them that you understand them. You are learning their guiding values be they rational, emotional or political. You're finding out what it is that inspires them.

They might not recognize their own hot buttons until you touch them in the pitch. But the hot buttons are there. Your task is to find them and access them.

While probing is essential, carrying it too far is prying. You are prying when you move into the wrong area (like not taking the hint), or probing at the wrong time, or wording the question thoughtlessly. A prober must know when to advance and when to retreat. Going too far is prying, not going far enough means you are forced to make assumptions about important issues.

Peter Rogen says that the best probing questions give the other person insights. They force the other party to think about problems from a new perspective. They can encourage the other person to think about a specific issue or area, to have their answers either add up inevitably as arguments that favour your organization, or at least set the stage favourably for you to make your proposal.

Pitch probing, at its best, helps others to think more about their own subject. This means using questions with creativity and with sensitivity.

TIP

Ask the criteria probe.

Another valuable question is: 'What are the criteria for judging the best supplier?' Follow-up with 'Why?' I will go to any lengths to get a copy of the written criteria which will be used by the client to assess the bids. Sometimes the client gives it out openly. Sometimes only some of the criteria are given. And, of course, there are some who do not know what criteria they use.

TIP

Personal versus professional.

Much of the communication we have is between 'roles' rather than between the 'real' person, the 'self'. As a result clients tend to answer questions from the company's point of view rather than from their own. Probe for personal opinion as well as their organizational stance. For example, on receiving a 'company line answer', ask another question: 'Yes, but how do you feel, Jim? What do you personally think about it?' or 'Taking your hat off as manager, how do you really feel about this?'

Don't let them hide behind the organization. You must get into their own minds, into their hearts. Find out what each person thinks. Find out how they feel. Do it with tact, but do it. You can end up being given information in confidence— sometimes vital information which other pitchers may not get.

You may also be able to create an ally in the client's camp. Information given in confidence by a prospect is a major winning signal. It means that your relationship is strong, perhaps stronger than your competitor's relationship. It's a positive sign that you're on the right track.

Relationships with the various players should be at an appropriate level. It can be too distant, thus missing out on sharing confidences, tips and so on, or it can be too close, and thus is affected by politics and you may suddenly find yourself sucked into the company's politics in a way which works against you.

TIP

Rational leads to emotional.

When interviewing, use rational questions to lead to emotional and political answers, for instance, 'Do you like the current service you are receiving?' If the answer is no, ask why not. 'Because I never see them. I want personalized service and I'm not getting it.'

Bingo! That's an important element to be included in the presentation. That's a guiding value which you have found.

Chapter 12

Tactics during the Lead-up

U SING THE WAR ROOM as a focal point for your pitch, you can more easily monitor the progress you are making. Be aware that you can use tactics to affect the environment leading up to the pitch, by preconditioning the client, and perhaps demoralising the opposition—or at least lowering their expectations. Here are 32 tactics—all used successfully, depending on the circumstances of the pitch.

TACTIC 1

In putting together your pitch team closely consider the client's organization and make sure that, in both pitching and servicing the account, you have found the appropriate matching of personnel. Each decision-maker and key influencer should have a corresponding person whom they respect and want to work with, but it should also be realistic and workable in the long-term.

So at all stages of the pitch, tag your key players to their key players, matching not only seniority, but also their character and styles and bearing in mind the long-term servicing of the account.

TACTIC 2

Questions with a hidden message.

The secret here is to make sure you ask questions that show an understanding of the organization and its issues, without asking the silly questions that prove you don't. The technical language must be right: are their sales representatives called 'reps' or 'territory managers'? Make sure you know before you go in.

TACTIC 3

Put a face to the name.

Often many of your presenters will not have met everyone on the client's pitch panel. If you can, get a photograph and pin it onto chart four in the war room (see Chapter 8 Getting on the Pitch List and Selecting Your Team), so people who may not have met someone beforehand will know them and be able to use their name when they do meet at the presentation. It is a comforting thing to be able to visualize to whom you will be talking. And being able to use first names on greeting helps rapport.

TACTIC 4

Keeping everyone honest!

Sometimes your organization may be starting behind the eight-ball. Other suppliers may have better contacts with the clients, or even existing relationships. You may catch wind of a competitor making claims which are unethical. If you find other suppliers are not playing fairly, or you feel you are being treated unfairly in the process of the pitch, take steps to fix it.

If I find a competitor is being unethical in the mistaken belief that 'all's fair in love and war' or 'business is business', I have no compunction about blowing the whistle on them. And doing it via the media is sometimes the easiest and most effective method. Befriend the media and use your journalist contacts to make sure that the right questions are asked of anyone playing unfairly.

TACTIC 5

Finding your weaknesses.

If a decision-maker happened to be talking to one of your competitors, what might your rival say to try to discredit you? Can you counter that claim?

TACTIC 6

Share experiences.

Throughout the probing process, take note of the ideas, feelings or experiences that you have in common with your client. In the past you may have shared an experience which left you both feeling great. By mentioning it in the presentation the client will recall those feelings and you'll find that rapport will naturally occur.

TACTIC 7

Oops!

One common mistake made by those pitching business, is to gleefully remind the client about something the client got wrong in the past. 'We know you had troubles with your New York office and we can make sure that won't happen again' or 'Your current advertising is being wasted'. For goodness sake, don't do it! The quickest way to destroy rapport is to remind them that you suspect they are inept. Leave it alone.

TACTIC 8

The one-meeting president.

Make the choice early as to whether it is appropriate for your biggest gun to be part of the interview process. If they are to get involved at this stage it could well have very positive results. It may impress the client. The downside is, of course, that the client may well expect your top person to stay involved in running the account after you have won it.

If you decide that you will score more points by having the top person involved, it is critical that they stay involved beyond one meeting. The one-meeting president syndrome is as bad as not having the president involved at all. Turning up once only sends the strongest signal that your president is there out of sufferance, not because they really want to find out about the client company and its issues.

TACTIC 9

Your place or theirs?

If the pitch can be staged at your own premises, so much the better. That will give you comfort with your equipment, your room, and control over coffee, lunch, telephones and client interruptions. If it has to be run at their premises, then make sure that you know their room like your own. Know the position of the light switches, the windows, the power points, the tables. Take a video camera and film their room, then show your presentation team what they will see on the day.

TACTIC 10

Matching levels.

Send a senior person from your team to meet a senior person on the prospect team. Before you call the meeting, check the level of conversation that you should have. Talk about matters that the client's senior representative is confident and knowledgeable about and deals with at their level. Do not force the client to talk about details which others 'below' them may be covering. If you persist, you will embarrass and/or annoy the prospect. Keep the discussion on major issues—the vision, the mission, the overall direction—not the cost of a bolt.

TACTIC 11

Predicting what the others will do.

Spend some time thinking about what your competitors will do in the actual presentation itself. Many organizations present predictably, that is, they always use overheads, they always follow a set structure, they use the same people. Try to predict what the others will do in their presentations—then either be better at it or different.

TACTIC 12

The need to be understood.

Probing is not just to get information which you can use to put your pitch together. It is essential to probe each person until they know that you understand their business. The pitch can often be won during this stage by building rapport, showing your interest, and finally proving that you have all the relevant information required to solve their problems.

Our research shows that 20% of decisions to appoint one organization over another are made on the basis of understanding the client's needs: 'They understood our business better than the others.'

TACTIC 13

Something for next time.

Each interview should end with an excuse to go back again. This excuse is critical to fostering further rapport and leaves the door open in case more is needed. Ask if the person would mind if you came back again to check any items which may still be unclear. The client will need to see you once, will be pleased to see you again, and will be pleasantly surprised to see you the third time. Now they understand that you are keen, that you are serious, and that you are focused on them.

TACTIC 14

It is not always possible to find out who will be on the final panel, but it is a crucial piece of information, so keep asking. Find excuses to get their names, for example. 'We want to personalize each copy of the document to leave behind. Knowing the names would make this possible.'

TACTIC 15

Comet or dark horse.

During the lead-up you can position your organization in several ways. You can, for example, promote yourself in the media and let it be known that you are the favourite to win the account— the strategy being to demoralize the competitors. You can also go to the other extreme and stay very very quiet publicly, while mounting a very heavy campaign of contact with the potential client. Let the competitors puzzle over your low profile. Have your suppliers sign confidentiality agreements. Avoid publicity when the media rings. The only profile that counts is the one you get once you have been awarded the business.

TACTIC 16

It's a combination of ideas, energy and actions.

Everything you do will make an impression—good or bad—not only within the presentation but during the process. It's another reason why everybody in your organization should be aware that the pitch is on and should know everybody involved on the client side. When the client rings to return your call, the receptionist can show recognition of the client, use the client's name and further build rapport.

TACTIC 17

Avoid nasty surprises.

Don't fall for the belief that it is better to keep your ideas secret until the presentation. 'Let's keep the big idea for last. Let's make it a huge surprise.' The dangers of this strategy often outweigh the benefits. A great idea delivered during the presentation may win the account—but it can just as often prove that you have no understanding of the client business. It is usually very hard to find a magic solution in three weeks when the client has battled the problem for months or years. Swallow your ego and bounce ideas off key members of the selection panel during the weeks leading up to the presentation. If you can get access to one panel member, then foster a relationship with that person by feeding ideas to them and getting opinions. If you have chosen the right person, one who has no hidden agenda, then you can often get reliable feedback which will show any pitfalls in your ideas. Modify them to make sure they will work.

Now, when you present the concept during your presentation you know that it will work and that it has been fine-tuned for maximum effectiveness.

TACTIC 18

Don't knock post-rationalization.

Post-rationalization has become the butt of many in-agency jokes. If you can't find a great strategy which develops into an awesome creative execution, then look for an awesome creative execution and post-rationalize a strategy which fits it. It's certainly done a lot by agencies. It sometimes is the creative way to find the right strategy.

Don't treat post-rationalization as an unethical practice. Try it when you hit a strategic brick wall. It may provide the key to unlocking a strategy. And, in reality, it is no different to having a vision first, then finding the way to reach it.

TACTIC 19

Send them something.

Is it timely or appropriate to send the client something in advance of your presentation? For example, you may decide that you will not have enough time in the actual presentation to provide the degree of detail you need. Why not send in advance the credentials part of your presentation, bound in a folder with a covering letter saying something like: 'Dear..., When we present to you on... we want to spend as much time as possible talking about your needs. To this end we have decided to send you, in advance, the background information about us. In this way we can devote the entire presentation to you and the challenges we will face together.'

TACTIC 20

Shooting down.

Are there ideas which your competitors could have which you can shoot down? If there are, then you might build a little time into your presentation to show how you explored certain strategies, then rejected them for obvious reasons. Then let your competitors present the strategies. You have now prepared the client to reject them. Field–Marshall Rommel once said: 'Never interrupt the enemy when he is doing something wrong.' You can add to that: 'Never miss an opportunity to make the client aware of faults in others' thinking.' (Of course, we will always do it with tact and good sportsmanship.)

TACTIC 21

Send them a clue.

It is very possible to modify the client's expectations by sending them something which gives them a hint or clue about your topic: perhaps a short video, a press clipping or two, a testimonial. Remember, the pitch started when you decided that you wanted to win this client. It doesn't begin when you start formally presenting.

TACTIC 22

Starting and stopping rumours.

Give consideration to the power of rumours. Some industries leak like sieves and rumours run rampant. After one pitch we were put onto the short-list for the final presentations. We knew that others would be wondering how we got onto the list. So we mentioned loosely in one or two hotels and restaurants, that we had come up with a great piece of creative from our New York office. Within days we had heard the rumour back.

We once spread a rumour that we had presented a creative idea successfully in round one of a pitch, against the guidelines laid down by the client in his briefing document. Within 24 hours a competitor rang the client and angrily demanded the right to present his creative. The client quickly pointed out that no such thing had happened and demanded an apology from the competitor.

If you wish, you can seed a rumour or two to distract or confuse your competitors. Use the industry, feed from it and feed it, seed it with comments which will be passed on. And be just as aware that the other suppliers may be doing the same thing.

TACTIC 23

Ask for a favour to test the relationship.

It started as an old 'tin men' sales trick. You dropped your pencil on the carpet during the meeting and if the client picked it up for you then that was a signal that you were doing well. I'm not suggesting that you run around dropping bags of pencils in front of clients, but sometimes it pays to ask the client tactfully for a special favour during the lead-up to the final pitch. You might ask for access to some research material, or ask if you could visit the factory, or seek interviews with special executives. If the client helps, then you are kindling a relationship. You can develop rapport in this way, but there is a proviso. If you ask for too much or cross the boundary of tact, then you are just as likely to harm the relationship.

TACTIC 24

The 'what's changed?' call.

Make a call a few days before the presentation. Ask the client if anything has altered since you last spoke. It's a way to pick up last minute changes that may have occurred. It's also a way to keep rapport going and it demonstrates your professionalism.

TACTIC 25

Clients can speak badly about their own organization, but they don't want you to.

As part of the probing process, we often sit and listen as individual executives in a client company speak candidly and harshly about their own organization and the mistakes it makes. They can list all the things which other executives have done wrong, they laugh about the poor results, they ridicule corporate decisions and even products.

Just listen and learn. Never agree and never build on their criticisms.

TACTIC 26

Seek ways to impress the client before the actual presentation.

This may consist of sharing some information with them, working in their company to learn the ropes, conducting research, interviewing their customers, or entertaining them at a non-business function. How can you been seen to be doing more, going further than the competitors?

TACTIC 27

Seek to get the best place on the pitch list.

Some people like to go first, some prefer to go last. Not many like to pitch second or third or anywhere else in the middle. It's an interesting theory, and I have won pitches from all positions.

In Monte Carlo the Sydney team were second up, after Berlin and before Manchester, Beijing and Istanbul. It was not ideal, but it gave us the opportunity to rehearse on the day at 8 am before driving to the Sporting D'Ete for the actual presentation. Berlin on the other hand had to be there at 8.30 am ready to go on at 9 am.

You can win the pitch from any position, but it is sometimes worth trying for a specific position in the order of presentations. For example, if there are six or more companies pitching and if each company has been allocated a long time, say, two hours, then the client has to sit through 12 hours of presentation information, much of which could be boring, much of which must be repetitious.

I would recommend trying to go first in that instance. You can arm the client to shoot down the companies which follow you. Your information will be fresh and new. The client may not have yet discovered the really difficult questions. They may use some of the things you say as the basis of questions to be used later. If appropriate, you might be able to provide the client with a checklist of questions and areas to be used to judge each company. If you go last, barely touch on anything which others will have covered already. Avoid repeating the client brief or profiling the target markets, unless you are sure that nobody else has done it already. Be different, be as bright as possible. And be fast.

TACTIC 28

Use the press to promote your cause.

Use timely Public Relations to publicize your organization. For example, an article promoting your expertise in a given area might help to raise the awareness of the client, either about you and your organization, or about the issues. While the pitch process is occurring, the client's team is still reading papers and magazines, listening to the radio and watching television. If it just happens that your organization is featured speaking authoritatively and creatively about issues which affect the client's business sector, then your presentation has already started. Better still, your opponents are not presenting against you at that time.

TACTIC 29

Find ways of meeting the client.

During the pitch process leading up to the final presentation, find ways of 'accidentally' meeting the client team members. Turn up at conferences, in hotel foyers.

The Sydney Olympic Games pitch team spent hours sitting in hotel foyers hoping to get a few seconds or minutes with an IOC member. It paid off for them.

One advertising executive, having been told that his company would not be keeping a major account, sat for two days in the foyer of the client's office until the CEO finally agreed (out of embarrassment) to see him. The agency went on to win the business against the predictions of all in the industry.

TACTIC 30

Involve the whole team.

Get your whole organization involved. Everybody from the most junior member to the chairperson knows the pitch is on and is excited by the challenge. The whole company is behind the presentation team, willing its members to win. Some organizations seem to keep new business as the precious domain of a few people in the company, and in some unfortunate companies (those which leak like sieves) this may be necessary, but it is far better to brief your entire team.

TACTIC 31

Check as you go.

If you have sufficient rapport, it may be possible to check your proposal with one of the key players. If you can do so safely, and by doing so foster further rapport and support, then do not hesitate.

This will help offset the presentation blunder that I call the logic leap. This occurs when the bidder does not see the client between the initial brief and the final presentation. At the time of the brief, both client and bidder are at the same point in their thinking. But what happens next is interesting—the client's thinking changes little over the following days leading up to the final presentation. But the bidder goes away and starts brainstorming for solutions. The pitch team meets and tries options, rejects them, tries new ideas, rejects them, moves their thinking in new directions—often far from the initial brief. By the time the final presentation comes around, the presentation has evolved beyond the initial thinking shared with the client. The mistake is to present the new ideas without bearing in mind that the client's thinking has not changed since that first meeting. To go ahead blindly and present brave new thinking means running the risk of losing the client completely.

You have two choices. The best is to keep communicating with the client as your thinking evolves use the changes in thinking as talking points to go back and discuss with the client. Then, by the time you do present, you know that the client will understand. The second choice is to spend valuable time in the presentation updating the client on everything you have done since the briefing, and on how your thinking has evolved. It can work equally well, provided you have enough time. The benefit is that the client can see how your team's strategic thinking works. The drawback is that without the ability to check with the client the new directions you have taken, you may go down a path which is simply wrong in the client's eyes.

TACTIC 32

What can you do that will make you stand out from all the others?

During the lead–up, constantly think about how the competitors might present. What can you do that will make your bid stand out from the others? Can you change the venue? Use different visuals? Bring in a guest speaker? Use music? Keep an open mind on suggestions that will make you more memorable than your competitors.

MATCHING THE ANSWERS

Asking the questions is one thing, but comparing the answers is even more fascinating. Bring the questionnaires back to the war room and take one question at a time, comparing the answers given by each person. By matching the results of the questionnaires you will find areas of confusion. Members of the selection panel will have different priorities and different attitudes, and will use different language. Discuss the answers that each person has given. Plot the results on the war room walls. When confusion exists, use this information to go back and get further clarification. Add to or modify each listener's chart.

Not only do you gain the information you need to win, but the probing process delivers another valuable reward. By the end of the second or third meeting it may be possible to have convinced each person that you understand more of their business than do your competitors. That can be 20% of the victory in its own right.

As the pitch progresses, the war room will be gradually filling up with information. And as it builds, you need to keep checking that you have covered all the bases.

OTHER SOURCES OF INFORMATION

You will also be adding information from sources other than client executives. 'Long-term' research can be carried out over weeks or months—if you have weeks and months. It can certainly be tackled in the days and hours leading up to the presentation itself.

There are several sources of information that you can explore to find the gems you need. Read material the organization has published recently, such as annual reports, newsletters, advertisements, trade mailers, direct mailers, brochures, proposals and reports. Study them for the terminology used, for comments by management, for tips about company practices, core values, long-term plans, disruptions, take-overs, buy-outs, financial trends, new products, personnel changes, curriculum vitae, company premises—any information which you can use to establish rapport and show the individuals in the audience that you have an understanding of their business.

Organize a press clipping service to check what may have been published about the organization. When a big enough competitive pitch is on, the papers and the trades are often interested enough to run scuttlebutt and facts. In some cities there are information services run in conjunction with large publishing houses and libraries. Subscribe to them.

Talk to other non-competitive suppliers who deal with the organization to which you are presenting, for instance, public relations consultancies, advertising agencies, couriers, retailers, wholesalers or manufacturers. Network through them.

If the organization is a public company, ring the Stock Exchange and one or two stockbrokers for information about the company's financial performance.

Check with your colleagues and friends in case anybody knows someone in your audience. I ran a pitch once in which we had a great deal of trouble finding out about the client's CEO—until we discovered that our receptionist had gone to school with his daughter. We paid for her to have dinner with her old friend, and told her of our situation. The daughter thought it was a lot of fun and she found out what we needed.

Ring the editor and advertising managers of the trade magazines which cover that particular industry or trade.

Ring business journalists who might know about the organization. Ring the client's secretary and receptionist and enquire if they would ask the decision-maker and key influencers for a curriculum vitae. Do it tactfully.

Look for non-business contacts at sporting and service clubs and chat to them.

All these sources can lead to prized information to go up on the war room walls. You never know, suddenly among all this prospecting you may uncover a piece of gold.

Once you have exhausted all your opportunities for analysis, you can still keep learning about the audience if you take advantage of last-minute opportunities before the actual presentation. Visit the presentation venue and check all the equipment. While doing so you can often talk to at least one member of the audience—use the opportunity to check final points. Telephone the client the day before the pitch to check final arrangements. Chat generally about how people feel, cross-check any points you need to have clarified. Arrive early and see if you can have coffee and a chat.

I have deliberately devoted a great deal of space to the whole subject of audience analysis, rapport building and probing, but I did so for good reason. Most pitches are won or lost before the presentation. Audience analysis is one of the most common omissions in a presenter's preparation and, due to the lack of awareness of the audience needs, the presentation is not tailored, does not have the desired effect on the audience and the result of the presentation is that nothing happens.

But, as I've shown, there are questions to ask and places to look for answers. The rest is hard work. The pay-off is a winning presentation.

Chapter 13

What's your Objective?

WELCOME TO DANGER TIME! You now have collected so much information that you run the real risk of losing focus. Brainstorm the problem in the war room. Go right back to the original question: 'When we have won the pitch, what will the decision-makers give as the reasons for our appointment?' Imagine your client attending a cocktail party with their business peers two weeks after appointing your organization. A colleague turns to your client and asks why your organization was appointed. What is your client going to say? What are the one or two reasons, rational or emotional or both, that they will use to convince a colleague? These are the take-outs that you need to ensure flow from your presentation.

A great way to check that your team is staying on target during the preparation for the pitch is to openly discuss each person in the power map—their roles and, importantly, their real needs. Cross-check these against what you have learned. At this stage, the most valuable person on your team will be the person able to sort out the valuable information from the dross. Discard the rubbish, focus on the strongest information. If there are gaps, then go back and fill them. If you can't go back, try elsewhere. If you can't try elsewhere, make your best judgment.

The presentation is drawing near and it's time to give serious consideration to what you feel you can achieve on the day. At first glance the answer is obvious: 'We will win the business', but that's not always the case. The presentation itself is just a stepping stone in the new business pitch. It is often the last step, but more often it is only one more step, followed by negotiation, perhaps another presentation, one-on-one discussion and legal contracting. So what do you want to achieve with the presentation?

The pitch itself can have a variety of objectives and, as the information flows in, and the client's and the individual's needs become clear, it is time to set your objective, if it is not already obvious.

TIP

Making your organization effective.

Imagine an organization in which something happened as a result of every meeting, every presentation. Imagine if executives left every meeting with something to do as a result of the meeting. This organization is the effective organization, the winning, focused organization. And clear objective setting in meetings and presentations can help achieve that situation.

The sad truth is that most meetings end with matters unresolved, inconclusive discussions held, confused participants leaving even more bewildered. The objective of the meeting was never set and therefore reaching it became a non-issue.

I remember having a meeting with the chairman of a potential client some years ago. He was in a hurry and as he sat down he said, 'What's the objective here?' Having requested the meeting and done my planning, I replied, 'The objective is to let you know why we should be chosen for the XYZ account.' He said, 'No, what is the objective?' I replied, ' To talk about the strategy.' He said (now getting angry) 'No, I want to know the objective. What do you want me to do as a result of this meeting?'

Presentation objectives are about having the audience *do* something as a result of the presentation or meeting.

The objective of your presentation is not to tell the audience about your organization. The objective is not to show them the solutions you propose. And the objective is definitely not to explain what they have been doing wrong. They are all subjects. Your objective is found by asking yourself: 'What do I want this audience to do as a result of this presentation?'

TIP

Less is more.

Imagine, you've been working at your pitch for six weeks. You started off with all the best intentions to focus solely on the key points, on the take-outs. But now it is three days before the presentation and you've started to panic. Panic habitually results in feeling the need to add words, rather than edit them out. And, frankly, it's the wrong way out of your dilemma. The only focus, three days before a pitch, should be on cutting words out. Less is more.

I sat in a pitch rehearsal for ten million dollars worth of advertising and for 20 minutes we had argued—pitch doctor against presenter—the pitch doctor saying to cut words out, the presenter saying that the client needed to hear those words. Finally, an old ad man in the corner, who had been asked to come and watch the rehearsal, leaned forward and said in a quiet voice: 'This entire segment of the presentation will not win or lose the business. Get rid of it.' In one fell stroke we removed 45 minutes of aimless talk. The pitch was delivered beautifully and the business was won. Whether it

continued...

> would have been, with the additional words, will never be known. But I doubt it.

As a business pitcher the aim is to have the listeners make a decision or accept a course of action, as proposed in the presentation. You may want them to buy your product or service. But it's not always the case. Perhaps you only want them to agree to discuss the subject further at another meeting. Perhaps you want them to consider your organization when they next look for suppliers.

Whatever the objective, it inevitably involves a change. Something has to happen to the audience. You have to affect them. They have to be different at the end of the presentation. If you have not affected the listeners, you simply haven't been effective.

Sometimes you will tell the audience your objective and, at other times, it will be for your knowledge only. So ask yourself: 'What do I want this audience to do as a result of this presentation?' When you are on the short-list for a piece of new business, and are making the final presentation, getting the right answer to that question is even more crucial.

This is where most teams make their biggest pitching mistake. They think the only objective is to provide the potential client with the best solution to the problem, as stated by the client. That could not be more wrong. The fact is that on most occasions you do not have time to find the best solution to the client problem.

The client may have spent years trying to fix it. If you can do it in three weeks, between receiving their brief and pitching, you are quite remarkable.

Secondly, often the correct solution will *lose* you the business. The solution is unpalatable, distasteful and the client doesn't want to hear it. So if you happen to be the organization which suggests this distasteful solution, you may be shot down like the messenger bringing bad news. They won't like you, because you are telling them what they hoped they would not have to hear. Instead they will associate you with negativity.

Your objective must be to win the business. It's that clear. It's not to give them the solution, unless the solution, so given, will win you the account.

If you are pig-headed enough to believe you have to give them the bad news regardless of the effect it will have, the net result will be that you are not appointed and therefore you never get the chance to solve that client's problem.

If you had been appointed, then you would have had the opportunity to discuss the client's problems in depth and at length, and then you could have fixed the problems—perhaps. But because you blew it in the pitch, you lost the pitch and you never had the chance. Not only did you lose, but the client lost too.

The sole objective of any pitch is to have the client appoint you as a result of your presentation. That's it. It's not to give the right solution, unless the right solution is also the winning solution. Save the tough calls for later when your team has had a real chance to study the problem and the options.

Of course, in an ideal world you have the right solution and the client would love it. So what do you do if you know that the only solution is the one which will be so distasteful to the client that you will lose? Instead of pitching the details of this unsavoury solution, you should instead set out to prove that you are the best organization to find the solution with them.

I have seen too much business lost by presenters setting out to demonstrate that they have a clever and complex solution, however distasteful, and they insist on berating the potential client with this solution. So choosing the objective is not always easy. You'll need to think deeply about it and, when you have decided on the specific objective, write it out in one sentence—clear, direct and precise—and without any negatives.

The objective should be practical, sensible, attainable and *measurable*. After the presentation you will be able to judge its success by whether the listeners did what you wanted them to do.

TIP

Staying relevant.

During the planning of the presentation, keeping the specific objective in mind will help you stay relevant and to the point. By keeping the objective up on the war room wall, you'll be able to limit your supporting material to that which is really meaningful. For example, if your objective is to get a decision, with the need for immediate implementation, you would probably include the method of implementation in your presentation. But if your objective is only to get a favourable response and there is no need for immediate implementation,

continued...

you may elect to save the methods of implementation for another meeting.

Objective setting is not a lengthy part of the planning process—it is asking and answering one simple question. But getting the objective right provides the focus you need to make things happen. It is the difference between being ineffective and being effective.

Chapter 14

Pitching your Credentials

TWO MAIN FORMS OF PRESENTATION play a role in winning new business. The first is the 'credentials presentation' which enlightens the client about your organization and what it offers. It is usually based on little or no briefing materials and tends to happen very early in the pitch process. The second is the pitch itself, which tends to be based on fuller orientation and includes solutions and detail. The focus is very much on the client.

From my experience, the traditional credentials presentation is delivered appallingly! In the cold light of day the concept of presenting your credentials to virtually total strangers is almost laughable. It simply tries to achieve too much in too short a time in the riskiest of environments. And when you read it as I have written it down below, it seems preposterous.

In around one hour you want the prospective client to get to know you and your team so well that they will put you onto a short-list to spend $X million of their money. In those 60 minutes you will give the client a coffee, introduce the client to the team, have their team members meet yours, establish rapport, settle everyone down in the presentation room, clear their minds of distractions, then grab their attention in a memorable way.

During those 3600 seconds your team will also endeavour to establish rapport, in order to prove that you know what you are doing. You'll have a case study or two, a slide of your offices around the world, an organizational flow chart, a list of your clients, a testimonial or two and perhaps a short film. By the end of the hour, you will have tried to sell the client your team, your strategic thinking, your creativity, your technical expertise, your financial credentials—and of course your fee structure. As a finale, your CEO will show why the client's account is a perfect fit for you. All the rest of the hour will be available for questions.

That presentation is a recipe for disaster. It isn't until you see a typical credentials pitch written down in all its complexity that it really shows itself in its true colours—as being totally unworkable and at least slightly ludicrous.

You cannot achieve all that in one hour—you cannot do it in a day. And you definitely cannot do it with total strangers! What is needed is something quite different.

Credentials presentations should not be 'credentials' presentations. Credentials or capabilities can be given in a document. The objective of a credentials pitch is to develop trust and interest in you as a potential supplier. And yet some suppliers will bury the client in facts and figures, charts and research, selling only to the head when it is emotion that is really needed.

If you only have one hour, then spend it doing what is absolutely essential:

+ show the client you understand their business;

+ show the client you will be great to work with; and

+ show the client they can trust you.

The reality is that you cannot even achieve that much in one hour, unless you do a lot in advance. So the credentials presentation must not be the first time you meet the client. If it is, then you cannot hope to show an understanding of the business.

That sounds obvious, but I know a case where the head of an agency rushed into the boardroom, made an impassioned presentation and left, having pitched wholeheartedly to one of his own agency's new account directors.

Presenting to strangers puts you in the lottery business. You have the same odds of picking the tone and mood as you would have of getting six winning numbers in lotto. It is virtually impossible to say the right thing because you don't know what they think or know about the subject.

In short, you will not achieve rapport unless you read the audience with the intuition of a fortune-teller. And, even if you are successful, rapport lasts one second if you say the wrong thing.

The credentials presentation should be a confirmation that the client made the right choice in inviting you to pitch. It should be the culmination of days, weeks or months spent getting to know the client, probing and listening, coming to a mutual respect or rapport.

By achieving, in advance, a level of rapport and knowledge of each other, you can spend the credentials presentation doing one thing—talking about each other as people about to form a long-term relationship based on trust.

The traditional agenda for a credentials presentation consists of 95% talking about yourself and 5% in questions. A better agenda is 30% on yourself and 70% talking about the client business and the future relationship. The credentials pitch is about what you can do for them, not what you have done for others. That means the credentials facts, figures and statistics should go mainly in a document.

The traditional credentials presentation involved an organization describing itself to a potential client. It was that easy. This is who we are. This is what we do. But it was obviously flawed, because the potential client only wants to hear what you can do for them.

As I have mentioned, the best credentials pitch is a confirmation that the right choice has been made in previous meetings. It is an affirmation of the client's decision to want to do business with you.

If the pitch scenario allows it, by the end of pitch the client should either have appointed you, or it will have put you onto the short-list of prospective suppliers—with an emotional head start over your opposition.

Throw away your stock credentials presentation. It's an insult to the people to whom you are presenting. It says that you couldn't be bothered tailoring it for them. Destroy the carefully honed video which you use for other pitches, forget about your company history, your client list, your billings, your organizational structure. Toss them away and start to think only of what benefits you can bring to this potential client.

Quickly you will find that you don't know enough about what they do to be able to find how you can help them. So call meetings, interview people, find out what they need and how they think.

During the credentials presentation you need to be able to prove that you understand their business better than the competitors. Show them that you want their business more than your competitors want it. Show them that you have a work ethic by demonstrating how you have done much more, gone much further than your competitors.

The best credentials pitches I have seen are short and incredibly effective. The lead presenter introduces the team and tells the client what the team is going to demonstrate. Each presenter then proves a part of that earlier claim. Then the lead presenter summarizes and asks for the business.

The client leaves remembering one, two or three things about your organization—the things you wanted remembered—the things which show you have the right credentials and attitude to solve the client's problems.

Up front you give three or four powerful points about how you can help the client. The points are not boastful or arrogant, because they have been chosen very carefully and based on the information you have already gathered during the process of meeting the client. The points are relevant and powerful. They impress the listeners. They have an effect.

Because these points are relevant and powerful and effective, the client wants to discuss them. So you spend the rest of the time doing just that. Because you have encouraged the client to speak, they feel more important and like you for it.

During the presentation, when an important question is asked about your organization, have a member of your team answer it, using visual aids if necessary. Put topics into manila folders with the visual aids needed to provide the answers to questions. When a question is asked, pick up the folder and demonstrate the answer concisely.

If the client asks if you have ever done similar work, then answer the question with a relevant case study. If you are asked about your buying power, demonstrate it. If the client doesn't ask anything, then have well-chosen, astute questions ready to ask them. Prepare questions which lead naturally to one of your organization's strengths. That sounds silly, but it means just that—don't ask questions which lead to somewhere you don't want to be.

Those who pitch a lot of business know that it is not this easy. You do not always have time to research a client. Often they seek a credentials presentation in two days. Often they refuse to let you discuss the business with anyone else in the organization. The excuses are always there, but the fact is simply this—the winning suppliers tend to know the client better than the losing suppliers.

The secret to winning the credentials presentation is to find out what is in the minds and hearts of each person in the audience, then evaluate the relative importance of each person's feelings in respect of getting your organization to the top of short-list. Then during the presentation, tap into the feelings and needs of the decision-makers and key influencers, and demonstrate that they can trust you to find the answers.

This is the right way to make a presentation about your organization's credentials. The client may have stated that they want to hear about you, but the reality is different. They really want to hear about what you can do for them.

The usual objective for the credentials presentation is to get you onto the short-list to pitch for the client business. But it is also more than that. The best objective for a credentials presentation is to have your organization appointed right then and there. And it can be done. If your presentation is so advanced in its research and client knowledge, if it gets the client to think about things from a new perspective, if it so impresses the client that they can think of nobody else, then you can win the business on the spot.

Even if your credentials presentation is only good enough to get you on a short-list of suppliers to make a full pitch, you can get on the list in a range of positions. You could find yourself as the hot prospect most favoured by the client or as just another supplier—the choice is yours, based on how much time and effort you put into the credentials pitch.

TIP

Advertising agency credentials.

Below is a typical flow for an advertising agency presenting its credentials. It can easily be modified for any organization by replacing some of the body segments.

◆ Team leader:
Welcome. Introduction of team (by name and role in agency—not role in presentation);
length of presentation;
question strategy;
creative opening;
subject/purpose;
agenda

◆ Section one—situation analysis:
general industry situation;
client's situation in context;
key issues for client;

continued...

criteria needed for the agency servicing this client.

◆ Section two—agency credentials:

agency overview;

strategy with examples;

creative ideas with examples;

media with examples;

mini-conclusion (how we meet the criteria so far).

◆ Section three—structure of agency:

resources;

people;

process of running major accounts;

costs (generally);

how we meet the criteria.

◆ Summary:

team leader reiterates key points.

◆ Conclusion:

team leader closes and asks for the business or to be involved in the next step.

Chapter 15

Structuring

the

Presentation

T HE BUSY MANAGER RUSHES OUT OF HER OFFICE past her secretary and tosses a sheaf of notes onto her desk. 'Type those up, please', she blurts as she dashes off to a meeting. Unfortunately, the secretary was in the middle of a letter at the time and missed the communication, so she carried on and the notes lay in her in-tray for a day.

The reason for this common form of miscommunication was that the manager did not check that the secretary was ready to receive the communication, she did not communicate accurately, and she did not check that the communication had been received and understood.

If the manager had first said the secretary's name, thus gaining her attention, then paused and delivered the instructions, then asked for a sign of her understanding ('Is that clear, Doris?'), the communication would have been clear and effective.

Good communication takes a little longer, but saves time in the long run. Remember these key points about communication:

1. Make sure the listener is ready to receive the communication.
2. Communicate.
3. Make sure the listener has received and understood the com-munication.

These three basic rules of communication organization form the basis of all presentation structures. The structure which is outlined in Chapter 14 and in more detail below is an expansion of those three basic principles of clear communication. And you should apply them to every form of presentation, from an impromptu chat in a lift or over coffee to a three-day conference.

STRUCTURING THE PRESENTATION

By now you should understand your audience thoroughly and have a clear objective set. You have collected all the information that you feel you need—probably, in fact, more than you need. Now you must decide what you are going to say first, second, third and last. It's a part of the process which thwarts many people, but it shouldn't.

Here is a structure which works for any presentation. It is one of a dozen which Rogen International uses, and it can be modified to suit all occasions:

+ opening remarks;

+ creative opening;

+ subject;

+ agenda;

+ body;

+ summary; and

+ conclusion.

TIP

> Give them the unexpected.
>
> Why present in traditional order? Advertising agencies, for example, tend to present strategy and creative ideas before the media strategy. Why not change that? Present the most exciting aspect first, or last, but make the decision based on potential impact, not on tradition.

Chapter 6 examined the role of communication. The basics of communication should drive the structure. Everything has a beginning, a middle and an end, and this is the cornerstone of a structured presentation. Not only does the entire presentation have a beginning, middle and end, but so does each section of it. If God is in the detail, the magic is in the structure.

Of the broad areas outlined above, the first four (opening remarks, creative opening, subject and agenda) prepare the audience to receive the communication. The key messages are received during the fifth area (the body) and the last two areas (summary and conclusion); they ensure the audience has received the communication and knows what it has to do about it.

OPENING REMARKS

At the beginning of the presentation, the presenter faces an audience which may or may not be ready to receive the communication. Coffee has possibly been served, or is still being served. The mind of each listener will be filled with similar or quite different distractions: 'How long will this take?', 'Will I be able to ask questions?', 'Should I take notes or not?', 'Who is that stranger sitting down the front?' and so on.

As the first pitcher, your team leader needs to take control because, if this isn't done promptly, then the most senior client member may do it for you. Presenters can clearly demonstrate their degree of control by the manner in which they open the meeting and begin the presentation; just as they will show control later by the way they handle interruptions and questions, the way they lead the discussion and conclude the presentation.

Opening remarks serve to establish who is in control, that is, who is starting, changing and stopping things; and they begin the process of preparing the listeners to receive the communication by clearing their minds of distractions.

Start by indicating that the meeting is under way: 'Let's begin.' If the meeting is being held at your premises, then it is appropriate to welcome the members of the client team and introduce the people on your team. But don't introduce them in terms of the role they will be playing in the presentation. Save that for your agenda. Instead, introduce them according to their role in your organization and give some background on each member, their length of time with your team if that is a benefit, and their expertise in special areas if that is helpful. For example, 'Let me introduce the team. John Wilkins is our financial controller. John's been with us now for some seven years, and during that time has worked on some of the most important projects in your field.'

TIP

> Laying on the hands.
>
> Clients want to know that your team is a real team. Members of a real team like each other and show it in their behaviour. One way to prove physically that you are a team is to walk around the table as you introduce each team member. As you talk about each person, stand directly behind them and place your hands in a friendly manner on their shoulders, make a quick joke about them, show you are friends as well as colleagues.
>
> In an ideal pitch, your team will have met the client's team several times. But in the real world we know that is not always possible. You may have flown in a senior executive
>
> *continued...*

> from overseas, who has not met anyone on the client team. The client may have flown in someone new or introduced audience members at the last minute. Use the appropriate language when introducing or reintroducing your team.

That's the first distraction dealt with. Everybody knows everyone.

Now tell the client how long the presentation will take and mention how you handle questions.

QUESTIONS

You have several choices with questions. You can:

- ✦ take questions at the end;
- ✦ take them at any time;
- ✦ take them at a number of specific times; or
- ✦ take important questions during the presentation and the rest later.

Taking questions at the end will help create a one-way presentation. I don't normally recommend it. It gives you control, but risks leaving lots of unanswered queries, resulting in the audience not understanding parts of your presentation or being distracted for the largest part of your talk by something not understood at the beginning. Having questions at the end gives you control, but destroys rapport. If time is a major constraint, then it is a valid tactic. If not, I would not recommend this method.

Taking questions at any time is my favoured strategy, provided you have relatively loose time constraints. It encourages interaction, albeit at the risk of losing control. But the audience members are involved, and that is critical. It is a consultative strategy, two teams working together to the same goal. But watch the time. If the client starts talking too much, the deadline may go out the window, and you could be blamed.

TIP

> Give the time problem to the client.
>
> A proven technique for handling the problem of questions and time is to tell the client in your opening remarks: 'Time is totally in your hands. Our presentation runs for two hours. In that time we have built in around 15 minutes for questions. But please feel free to ask as many as you like.'

Taking questions at a number of specific times works well too. Tell the client that you will take questions at the end of each of the agenda areas. You will have control during each section, and can clarify matters at the end of each section. It combines interaction with control.

Taking important questions during the presentation and the rest later is another sound strategy. Delivered carefully, you can discourage open questions while ensuring that the client feels able to ask important questions. It limits the number of questions, while allowing the material ones. 'We have allowed time for your questions at the end but, of course, if you have an important one during the presentation, feel free to ask it.'

If there is a final strategy, it is to allow no questions. I don't think this is a valid strategy. It only serves to antagonise and sets a 'down' tone for the presentation.

As team leader you should choose the question strategy which best suits the tone and mood you wish to create.

Now that you have cleared away the possibility of the audience members not knowing if they can ask questions, or when, let your audience know if you have a leave-behind document and tell them you will give it out later.

Never, never, never provide your document to be read by the audience during your presentation. It's a guaranteed way to lose control. The accountant goes straight to the price, the marketer goes to the advertising, everyone has their favourite part of your document—and you are trying to keep their attention on your flow. Instead, say up front that you will be handing out a document at the end of the presentation. Then run the presentation according to your planned flow.

Having handled the administrative details of your presentation you now have a group of listeners which is only partly prepared to receive your communication. Each member of the audience knows how long you will take, who everyone is, whether they can ask questions, and when, if they have to take notes and so on. But there is still a way to go before they are ready to receive your message. You could argue that the presentation really hasn't started. You've handled the administrative details, but that's all.

CREATIVE OPENINGS

The next step is to wake them up to bring everyone into the present—to focus their attention on what you will have to say and to grab their attention. The device we use is the creative opening. The objective of the creative opening can vary: it may have the purpose of focusing listener attention onto your subject or objective; or setting a theme; or opening a line of thinking; or demonstrating creativity.

Relevance is mandatory.

Any creative opening must be relevant to the subject being discussed because, if it is not, you run the real risk of having the listeners remember the creative opening, but forgetting what it had to do with the rest of the presentation. For example, a very funny joke—if not relevant to the subject—will probably be remembered in lieu of the objective. The relevancy test is the 'bridge test'. If you can't link the bridge to your subject by following it with the words 'with that in mind...' or 'that brings me to my subject...', then your creative opening is not relevant.

The following paragraphs give examples of the most used creative openings.

A RELEVANT QUOTATION

The quote is probably the safest creative opening for your presentation. It can focus, motivate and inspire because it often links the more mundane issues being discussed in the presentation with the lofty words of the world's best thinkers. Some examples follow. Try to avoid quotes with possible sexist or racist overtones—you don't want to alienate your audience.

◆ To lead into the subject of 'problem solving':

'Everything should be made as simple as possible, but not simpler.'

ALBERT EINSTEIN

'An intellectual is a man who takes more words than necessary to tell more than he knows.'

DWIGHT EISENHOWER

✦ For a presentation on advertising:

'Our job is to bring the dead facts to life.'

or

'It took millions of years for man's instincts to develop. It will take millions more for them to even vary. It is fashionable to talk about changing man. A communicator must be concerned with unchanging man, with his obsessive drive to survive, to be admired, to succeed, to love, to take care of his own.'

or

'Whereas the writer is concerned with what he puts into his writing, the communicator is concerned with what the reader gets out of it.'

BILL BERNBACH

✦ On a major change:

'If there's not a ripple at the bow you're drifting.'

or

'If in the last few months you haven't discarded a major opinion or acquired a new one, check your pulse. You may be dead.'

GEORGE BERNARD SHAW

'You see things; and you say, "Why?" But I dream things that never were; and say, "Why not?"'

JOHN F KENNEDY

'Intelligence is knowing the right amount of force.'

or

'*Common man prefers comfort to pleasure*
Convenience to liberty
And a pleasant temperature
To that deathly inner consuming fire...'

HERMANN HESSE

◆   On motivation:

'*Success is not something you aim for,*
it is something your achievements attract.'

or

'*When you cease to dream you cease to live.*'

MALCOLM S FORBES

'*When it is obvious that the goals cannot be reached, don't*
adjust the goals, adjust the action steps...'

or

'*Nothing great was ever achieved without enthusiasm.*'

RALPH WALDO EMERSON

'*People ask the difference between a leader and a boss... The*
leader works in the open, and the boss in the covert. The leader
leads, and the boss drives.'

THEODORE ROOSEVELT

'*Our greatest glory is not in never falling, but in rising every*
time we fall.'

CONFUCIUS

'*Failure is only the opportunity to more intelligently begin*
again.'

HENRY FORD

'*A man without a purpose is like a ship without a rudder.*'

or

'It is not the critic who counts,
Not the man who points out how the strong man stumbled or
where the doer of deeds could have done better.
The credit belongs to the man
Who is actually in the arena;
Whose face is marred by dust and sweat and blood;
Who strives valiantly;
Who errs and comes short again and again;
Who knows great enthusiasms,
The great devotion,
And spends himself in a worthy cause;
Who, at the best, knows in the end the triumph of high
achievement;
And who, at the worst, if he fails,
At least fails while daring greatly,
So that his place shall never be
With the cold and timid souls,
Who know neither victory or defeat...'

THEODORE ROOSEVELT

✦ On public speaking:

'I do not object to people looking at their watches while I'm
talking. But I do strongly object when they start shaking them
to make certain they are still going.'

LORD BIRKETT

'Blessed are those who have nothing to say and cannot be
persuaded to say it.'

ANON

✦ On a marketing problem:

'Never interrupt the enemy when he is doing something wrong.'

ROMMEL

'For every complex problem there is invariably a simple solution—which is invariably wrong.'

or

'General notions are generally wrong.'

LADY MARY WORTLEY MONTAGU

Go to the library and borrow some books of quotations—Mark Twain, Bill Bernbach, Sun Tzu, Winston Churchill, Dorothy Parker—there are thousands of quotes, many of which are now available on software.

Make your creative opening powerful. Whatever the creative theme, it should be appropriate and powerful. It can sell at an emotional level. Maybe it will encapsulate the key take-outs from your presentation. Maybe it will make the client look at their problems in a new paradigm. Maybe it will show your insight into their business situation. The theme will give you freedom to use devices, quotes, visual aids, music and fun to lighten up your presentation.

Take the theme 'there are no simple solutions'. In this scenario our client was the incumbent in a five-way pitch for a multinational client. The obvious strategy for advertising was to use the power of the client's company name to sell the individual brands at brand level. That was the simple solution, but it was wrong as a pitch-winning strategy because the decision-makers were brand managers who wanted their own brand promoted above the company name.

We chose as a theme 'there are no simple solutions'. Our strategy was to knock out the obvious solution (and thus any agency which chose it) right up front. I had our CEO start the presentation with a quote, printed boldly on a piece of card:

> *'For every complex problem there is invariably a simple solution, which is invariably wrong.'*

He then went on to say that the simple solution to their problem was the one-image strategy, and then he showed why it was wrong. Having convinced them of that, he went on to prove that the right solution was in fact complex, but our agency had found the solution. We then revealed it over the next hour.

At the end of the presentation we returned to the quote and reminded them that the simple solution was not the right one.

Because we were the first agency to pitch, the others, several of whom had chosen the one-image strategy, found themselves facing an almost hostile audience when they revealed their strategy.

AN ANALOGY FROM HISTORY, SPORTS OR BUSINESS

By using a parallel for your subject, chosen from a category that interests the audience, you can help them cross the bridge from something they understand to something they might at first find difficult to comprehend.

Find a topic that's in the news, or something relevant that you once experienced or read about, such as a famous battle, a corporate take-over, a trial, a natural disaster, a great scientific discovery. Describe what happened, then bridge from it to the subject of the day.

The power of the analogy is that it is often better able to interest the listener and gain attention at this early stage of the presentation, than your subject might be.

GET THE AUDIENCE TO DO SOMETHING

Audience involvement is a sure way to make sure everybody is awake. A listener asked to do something must be focused.

We ran a new business presentation to a major bank, which had an internal communication problem. Our agency CEO put on a general's helmet and gave a similar helmet to the CEO of the bank, sitting on the other side of the table. Our CEO then whispered in the ear of the person seated next to him. That person whispered to the next and so on, until the last agency person whispered into the ear of the client CEO.

> OUR CEO: 'The message I sent was: "Send reinforcements, we're going to advance." What message did you receive?'
>
> CLIENT CEO: 'Send three and fourpence, we're going to a dance!'
>
> OUR CEO: 'That's what we believe is happening with your bank's internal communication. The message that leaves the top of the bank is being muddled en route to the front line. But we believe we can solve that problem for you.'

ASK THE AUDIENCE A QUESTION

Provided you can handle the answer, asking a question will involve your listeners and can lead them to your subject, for example, 'What is the single biggest question facing your industry in the next five years?'

USE AN IMAGINARY SITUATION

'I'd like you to imagine a situation in five years' time. Your industry has undergone some major changes. Business is done on the Internet; your sales force has been halved...' Project the client into the future and create awareness of the need for change.

SHOW A VIDEO

Video libraries provide dozens of videos designed to make a point which may be relevant to your topic. Shop around for an example which suits your purpose. Keep it very short—one minute or two—no longer. Go out and shoot video footage of interviews with the client's customers. Have them talk about the real opportunities which you have ascertained. Let the customer's comments change the perception of your audience, to prepare it for your solution.

TIP

The checklist opening.

It's an oldie, but a goodie. Open your presentation with the words: 'If we were in your shoes, here are the criteria that we believe your supplier must be able to meet.' Then show them a checklist of items, such as offices in every State, high service standards, fast delivery, top quality, ability to provide creative solutions and so on. (Make sure the checklist only includes criteria which your organization can meet.)

Leave the checklist up for the duration of the presentation. Then, during your summary and conclusion, refer back to it and check off each item with a bold coloured pen,

continued...

confirming that you have proven how your organization matches every criterion.

It's a powerful way to have the listeners focus on what you feel is important in the pitch. The physical act of checking off the items at the end of the presentation is a forceful example of how strong actions can convince an audience.

CHANGE THE VENUE

Choose a venue which makes your point. If the client is in fast-foods, mock up a fast-food outlet at the presentation venue. Companies have presented to truck manufacturers in the back of a pantechnicon truck, in aeroplanes, on boats, in restaurants and bars. Why only use your boardroom or theirs?

BUILD SOMETHING

Build a seesaw about a metre long and sit it on the desk in front of you and the client. Make one end of the seesaw 'the problem' and one by one stack building blocks on top of that end, each block representing a factor which is causing the problem, for instance, market share, price, quality and distribution. As you pick up each block, show it to the client and talk about the problem. Then add it to the pile—on the end of the seesaw.

Now move to the other end and talk about your solution. Pick up different coloured blocks, again printed with words describing aspects of the solution, like building the brand, sales incentives, tighter quality control and new marketing. As you pick up each block, talk about it and begin to build a pile on the other end of the seesaw. Suddenly, the weight of the new blocks will tip the scales and the seesaw will move into balance. The action is visual and kinesthetic proof that your solution works. Now put the seesaw to one side (still where the listeners can see it) and start the main part of your presentation. I've used the seesaw technique in three countries, for two wins and a loss.

The involvement in building something in front of the listeners makes this a potent technique.

BRING IN A GUEST

Sometimes a mystery guest stepping into the room or appearing on video may be the attention-grabber that you need to kick off your presentation. They may be the presenter you are going to suggest heads up a new advertising campaign, a spokesperson to endorse a new product line or a well known singer. Make sure the guest is relevant to the thrust and theme of your presentation, and introduce that person in a way which gives you a way out if they do not have the effect you desire.

 TIP

It's a creative opening.

I watched an organization rehearse for a major new business pitch for which they had created the theme 'it's war!' They used the conflict analogy to drive home the importance of the marketing war that the client was facing. To hammer home the point, the entire pitch team dressed as soldiers in uniform, with tin helmets. The creative opening certainly had

continued...

an impact, but then the presentation moved on to the details of the business problem and solution—and the presenters began to look slightly ridiculous still dressed in their soldier suits. Instead of their having made a strong point once, their garb became a distraction. The client stopped listening and started wondering if the pitch team was really serious. The lesson is that a creative opening should not continue in a fashion which makes it a distraction. Make the point and move on.

USE A PROP

An advertising agency presenting a tactical campaign might give the potential client an arrow, to show targeting. A computer company might ask the client to switch on a computer which then starts the presentation with its own display. A finance company might hand out abacuses and ask the client to use them to check the figures in the presentation. The prop involves the audience. It is tactile and thus adds another dimension.

INTRODUCE SOME UNEXPECTED PRESENTERS

We did a very creative presentation for a client that had neglected its target market. As our CEO introduced the team he added: 'There are four more people that are critical to our presentation today and I'd like now to introduce them.' He moved to four empty chairs and filled them one at a time by picking up full-colour foam cutouts of people—each representing a different person in the client's target market. He introduced each of them and described their buying habits and their lifestyle and then he bridged to how to maximize sales for XYZ by understanding the target market. The figures stayed in their chairs for the entire presentation as each presenter that followed involved them in the pitch by referring to them as they discussed advertising, promotion and media.

So now your opening remarks have cleared the listeners' minds of distractions and your creative opening has grabbed their attention. Now you use a transition to signal that you're moving to the next part of the presentation.

To link your creative opening to the subject, you have the choice of a host of phrases and clauses:

✦ 'That brings me to...'

✦ 'With this/that time in mind we'd like to discuss...'

✦ 'And in keeping with this...'

✦ 'In response to that I'd like to...'

✦ 'And this will serve to introduce our subject...'

✦ 'Our situation here is very similar to what we have just seen.'

Using transitions for logic and smoothness.

The use of linking phrases, clauses and sentences give your presentation a smooth flow. The transitions signal to the listeners that you have completed one part of the presentation and are moving to the next. The listeners are taken by the hand and led in comfort through the presentation, never wondering where they are, always being able to concentrate on the subject matter without distraction caused by 'getting lost or confused'.

The transitions will be added as part of the process of fine-tuning your script. If you are working without notes, then practise using them to bind your presentation components together.

SUBJECT

It is now time to name the purpose or subject for the presentation. Use a bridging phrase from your creative opening and then state the purpose of the presentation. It does not have to be a long-winded statement because one would hope that everyone knows why you are there anyway. In some cases it can even be ignored, but make sure that the listeners do understand what you are going to give them: 'So with that in mind, today we will show you...'

Choosing a subject for the presentation is an opportunity for creativity. Our research over many years shows that most winning presentations have a theme, rather than a bald subject, that is, it's a presentation with a specific direction and focus.

◆ 'Together into the Year 2000!'

◆ 'Making XYZ Number One!'

◆ 'Onward to $20 million dollars!'

◆ 'It's War!'

◆ 'A Global Strategy for a Global Airline.'

◆ 'There is no Simple Solution.'

◆ 'Lessons From the Past.'

◆ 'Messages from Sun Tzu.'

Giving your presentation a theme promotes creative scope which can be used throughout the presentation to bring highlights to otherwise dull subjects.

THE AGENDA

Now it's time to tell the client your agenda for the presentation. You'll recall that as part of your opening remarks you introduced your team by their titles and expertise, but I deliberately recommended not mentioning the roles they would play in the presentation. Now it's time to reveal their roles.

First you will need a transition, to add that fluidity and to signal to the client that you are moving forward. To link the subject/recommendation to the agenda, try using phrases like these:

✦ 'There are three key issues...'

✦ 'We're looking at this issue from three main aspects... (or from three fundamental points of view...)'

Now announce the roles. 'Terry will be discussing the market environment and the challenge which we face, Jane will present our strategy and Harry will look at how we will manage your account.'

TIP

> Make the agenda visual.
>
> Show the client the agenda on a flipchart, a slide or a board. Display the agenda and leave it up somewhere in the room so the listeners can cross-check occasionally if they have to. As you move from each agenda item to the next, do so by walking over to the displayed chart and pointing out where the presentation has reached.

Probably the most time-consuming part of organizing your ideas is selecting an appropriate agenda—deciding what areas you need to cover, in which order. The sequence of information you choose will depend on the audience and the amount and style of information you wish to convey. For example, you may decide on an analytical approach—the challenge is, our options are, our recommendation is.

You may choose the broader agenda of context, concept and form (market context, our solution and how we will manage it). This is certainly one agenda which works extraordinarily well for a multitude of credentials presentations and pitches.

You start by putting the client's situation into the wider context by discussing the economy, the market itself, the target audience, perhaps the client's competitors, the client's situation and actions, and the challenge or problem that has resulted. Then you summarize that section by defining the criteria for choosing a supplier which can meet the challenge. Then you move to the concept—that is, your solution—and you discuss each part of it. And finally you discuss the form—that is, how you will handle the logistics of the plan—perhaps ending with account management and costings.

Choosing an agenda is a weighty issue. It will affect the build of information, the way the client reacts, the level of interest at various times in the presentation. It can decide if you will release information dramatically (the big idea last) or in a logical build which educates the audience as you go.

A popular agenda is chronological. 'One year ago, the situation was ...and today it has changed to...tomorrow's challenges will be...'

If the final pitch is the culmination of several agendas, you may be able to go straight to the solution. 'Our recommended strategy... implementation...costs.' If you have been doing a great deal of research on behalf of the client, you may want to use something like: 'Research program overview...analysis...recommended solution.'

Select an agenda which suits your needs. It may have three, four or five different areas, and in some cases many more. But be aware that busy, direct listeners get turned off by very long agendas. You can always get a presentation into three or four broad areas.

BODY

At this point in your presentation, you have the listeners ready to receive your communication. You have cleared their minds of distractions with your opening remarks, you have grabbed their attention with your creative opening, you have told them the subject and the major issues your team will be covering. Now it's time to start the core of the presentation.

To link the agenda to the first part of the body, use another transition. It is a key signal that indicates you are starting the body of the talk. Say: 'Let's get underway...' or 'To begin with, Jane will be covering...' or 'To start with we have...' or 'So, moving to the first issue...'

TIP

Use a visual link.

A technique which has worked for me in the past is to have each presenter finish their presentations with a final slide on which the name of the next presenter is written. The presenter introduces the next speaker then sits down, the new speaker steps up and changes the slide to their first visual aid.

Each body part of the presentation will have its own beginning, middle and end. It will have its own opening remarks, albeit very short, its own creative opening, subject and agenda, body, summary and conclusion.

Don't neglect the sub-structures required to deliver even tiny parts of the presentation. The body should have a form, no matter how simple. As one president of an American agency told his team member during a pitch, 'For God's sake, tell me what you are going to be talking about, so I'll know what to expect.'

The conclusion which each speaker reaches at the end of their body segment must play a role in building the argument. It must be part of the overall theme. It adds a component of the argument, building towards a result which is simply indisputable.

As each speaker finishes, there is a transition to the next. It may be a formal transition handled by your team leader who takes the opportunity to make a mini-summary of what has gone on; it may be done with visuals; it may be nothing more than a hand-over as one person stands up and another sits down. The transition, however, should reflect the tone and mood and style which you have chosen.

TIP

*O*bviously.

I once heard a presenter say, 'The obvious solution is...'. She then revealed the proposed solution.

However, the client had tried that path a long time ago, and, for reasons not disclosed to the presenter, decided not to

continued...

adopt it. The last thing he wanted was to hear someone else—a person with little comparative knowledge of the problem—expound a facile solution.

Presenting such a resolution, without enquiring as to whether it had been tried, suggests that the client is a fool. That's not a great rapport builder. If the solution is so freely apparent, there will also probably be a reason why it does not work.

TIP

Show you're a team.

If you know there is a special need to show that you are a team, then use first names during the transition. 'Thanks, Ann.' If it works for you, pat the preceding speaker on the shoulder as they leave. The touch shows teamwork.

If you are handling the transition from one part of the presentation to the next, use a transition to link the first part of the body to the second part of the body, for example:

✦ 'Moving to our next area of concern...'

✦ 'Next we come to...'

✦ 'Now let's examine...'

✦ 'To continue the sequence we have...'

✦ 'Our next important element is...'

And so it continues, speaker by speaker. To link the penultimate part of the body to the final part:

✦ 'Finally and most importantly we have...'

continued...

+ 'Last, but certainly not least, we come to ...'
+ 'That brings me to...'
+ 'Finally then let's examine...'
+ 'Lastly we have...'

Each part of the body will be delivered in a persuasive manner using examples, statistics, facts, visual aids, testimonials and

SUMMARY

Once the last speaker has finished, it is the role of the team leader to stand again and summarize the key points made by each speaker. They will again use a natural transition to start the summary:

+ 'So we've seen...that...first...next...and finally...'
+ 'In a nutshell then...'
+ 'Looking back we see...'
+ 'So let's now take an overview...'
+ 'Reviewing then, we covered...and saw that...'

The summary is the most valuable, but most often overlooked, part of a presentation. It ensures that the listeners walk away with the exact key points you wish them to have. Without a clear, crisp summary of the main points, the risk is that the listeners will remember the wrong part of the presentation and will take away the wrong tone and mood. The summary lets them relax while you do the hard sorting for them. You find the main messages and you reiterate the important ones. You make it easy for them to get the point. The summary need only be short, but it is essential.

CONCLUSION

Now it's time to close. The conclusion reiterates the main point of the presentation and the next step or steps. To link the summary to the conclusion and recommendation, the team leader uses a transition like:

◆ 'Given that...'

◆ 'Therefore...'

◆ 'Consequently...'

◆ 'It follows conclusively then, that...'

◆ 'Having shown...I recommend that we immediately...'

◆ 'The thought I'd like to leave with you...'

◆ 'What I want you to take away from...'

◆ 'It's certainly beyond doubt that...'

◆ 'I strongly recommend...'

◆ 'I strongly urge...'

◆ 'Clearly our next step is...'

It may be as elementary as summarizing and concluding by saying: 'Today we have shown you that this is not a difficult problem. Terry showed that our research found two major areas of opportunity, in distribution and pricing. Ben outlined a strategy which addresses both in a very cost-effective manner by using the franchising system that our organization offers. And finally Jane showed that we can implement it in two months, throughout five major States, without your having to use any of your own resources. Given that, I strongly recommend that you approve our submission. Our team is standing by. If you are able to appoint us by Friday, we can have this system in place for you by January next year.'

Just as at the start of your presentation when you established control by making the opening remarks, now it's time to close the meeting. Thank the client team members for their time and attention and for any particular contribution that they might have made. Acknowledge that the meeting is over. If the meeting was successful, acknowledge that too. Hand out any leave-behind material. Invite those present for coffee or refreshments, if applicable.

The structure outlined is a classic model flow for a presentation. That is how the listeners will hear it delivered. But there is a slightly different way that you can plan it to cut time and keep your team focused.

A well run and well structured presentation conveys to your audience the thought that if your proposal or recommended course of action is accepted, you will execute it in the same well organized and effective way. A presentation with no beginning, middle or end, no point or apparent objective, gives the impression that if you won the business you would run it in a similarly inept manner. Plan your presentations to reflect the style of organization the client will want to run the business.

First I will show an order for planning your presentation and later in the chapter, I'll give you the flow as it would occur in the meeting itself. So, to start the process of organizing your ideas logically, take a clean full-size pad and leave a gap at the top of 10 or 12 lines. Then write down your subject. The subject may be a topic, purpose, or in some cases it may be the recommendation itself.

Now go to the bottom of the page and write down your conclusion. It's the main point of your presentation. It should also be what you are going to ask the listeners to do as a result of your presentation. It's the last thing you are going to say, with the possible exception of questions.

By writing down the conclusion so early in your planning, you have given your presentation an assured focus. Now everything you write must lead inevitably to that conclusion. If it doesn't play a role in building a logical argument leading to your conclusion, it doesn't have a place in your talk.

Now go back to the space under your subject and write down the agenda headings across the page from left to right forming three or four columns. These are the areas which you will cover to reach your conclusion logically.

Now take each agenda heading and list the key points of evidence you need to convince the audience. At this stage just use headings; for example, under the agenda heading 'situation analysis' you might have key point headings of:

✦ the economy;

✦ market overview;

✦ competitive analysis;

✦ target market analysis;

✦ the challenge;

✦ criteria for a solution.

You will flesh these out later as information is gathered.

Under each column write the word 'summary'. Scan each list of body items and select the main point or points from each. List them in the summary.

At this point the page is nearly full. You have virtually mapped out the total presentation. You will still need to fill out the details, but the flow is now organized. To add the finishing touches, go back to the space you left at the top of the page. Now think about your opening remarks and write down those introductory points you will make to clear the listeners' minds of distractions.

Finally, think of a creative opening idea and write it down in the remaining space between the opening remarks and the subject.

Now you have a structured plan for a winning presentation. Put it up on the war room wall and get each team member to take responsibility for their parts of the presentation. Each person may take an area of the body and will expand it with the detail required.

TIP

Pitch till they leave the room and then keep pitching.

Break out of the paradigm that says the presentation is limited to the confines of the presentation room. We have very successfully used the technique of redecorating our offices while the client team is in the presentation. As they file out to go home, they walk past displays which reflect the ideas they heard in the room. When they get back to their office, we have sent them a model, or picture, or an additional document. We keep pitching way past the end of the 'pitch'.

Chapter 16

Making it Persuasive

ANYONE WHO HAS BEEN FORCED to sit through a lengthy, tedious presentation, filled with buzz words, technical jargon and irrelevant material, will appreciate the importance of a tailored, persuasive message, which is succinct, targeted and objective-driven.

By now you have been accumulating information, sorting it, prioritizing it and, hopefully, throwing away anything that your audience does not need to hear. Now we need to turn the balance into persuasive language, instead of just words.

The first step is to write down the features of your subject. What are the key points of what you intend to say? Write them down in a column on the left-hand side of a piece of A4 lined paper.

Step two is to make those features relevant to the audience. Take each feature and ask, 'What does this mean to the listeners?' For example, the feature may be that the organization will introduce a new holiday rostering system. What it means to the listeners is that they will be able to choose to take their holidays at a time which suits them, rather than being forced to take holidays during quiet times.

The feature itself may not be very interesting, but what it means to the listeners is of great interest. In one step you have taken a feature and turned it into a benefit. Now it is relevant and interesting to the listeners. So ask what each feature you have written down means to the listeners—and write the benefits on the right-hand side of the page.

Step three is to prove your statement to the audience, and proof is having the right amount of the right kind of evidence needed to convince the decision-maker.

To convince the audience you therefore need to present evidence that what you are saying is true. And there are quite a few different types of evidence, depending on the motivational needs of the audience. The motivators will differ according to the actual needs of the listeners. For example, some will be motivated by purely rational reasons such as meeting budgets, fitting with long-term business strategies, achieving profit projections or cutting costs. Others will be moved by such emotional motivators as pride, security, fear, liking, trust, ambition, greed, love or respect. Think about which motivators are best for your particular listeners, then select the right amount of the right types of evidence you will use to convince them.

Our definition of evidence is that: 'Evidence is anything which supports your case'. It is a broad definition for very good reason. The very way in which you deliver your presentation will be evidence that you can deliver what you are promising. If your presentation is tight, focused, objective-driven and very professional, then that will help convince an audience that you can deliver. If, on the other hand, your presentation is loose, aimless, off-target and boring, it is hardly evidence of your ability to deliver anything.

Here are some types of evidence which fall under the broad heading of 'anything which supports your case':

✦   Irrefutable facts—for instance, your statement may be that your organization is very successful. The irrefutable fact is that you have made 35% profit every year for the past five years.

- Statistics—such as surveys, market research, audience ratings, trends. Use them to support your argument.

- Case studies and examples—you can, for example, quote successful relevant projects carried out for others.

- Testimonials—you can use testimonials from other end-users, from experts and from recognized institutions. Provided the listeners respect the person or institution giving the reference, then testimonials can be very powerful.

- Hypothetical examples—by giving the listeners an example in theory, you help establish that you understand how the process works and can therefore carry it out in practice.

- A strong visual aid—visualising your argument in the form of a graph or chart adds an authority which exceeds rational thinking. The fact that the figures are shown in an impressive chart, for some reason, adds importance and supports your case.

- Demonstration—such as an advertising agency showing its television advertisement reel to demonstrate its creativity, or a presenter holding up a product and demonstrating its benefits. I have demonstrated high level of intention and enthusiasm by having the entire supplier team walk into the presentation wearing tee-shirts with a message for the client. That's demonstration!

- Analogies—drawing an analogy with something which the listeners understand will encourage them to be persuaded by your subject.

So, once you understand your audience and what you want them to do as a result of your presentation, you then conceive of what will motivate them to accept your case. You collect the evidence to prove to them that you are right, and finally, you make sure that what you are saying contains benefits for the listeners.

What else can you do to make the presentation even more convincing? Here are tips we've used with great success over many years.

TIP

Make the client guilty.

Give them evidence of your industry. Show how much work has been done to win the account. Make sure the client realizes just how many hours have gone into it. If this is done tactfully, then you can almost make the client believe they will feel guilty if they do not appoint you.

TIP

It's what you leave out that makes it great.

Chinese philosopher Sun Tzu said: 'I hear and I forget, I see and I remember, I do and I understand.' Sometimes you need to go through the process of research and analysis before you really understand it. But does the client really have to sit through it again? The chances are they already understand a great deal of what you are showing anyway. If they do, then just get to the point of each issue. Cut out the revisiting of issues.

TIP
TIP

Give them permission to believe.

Sell to the heart. It's been a successful advertising objective for years: 'Drive a bulldozer through the heart.' The heart buys, the head rationalizes. So your pitch first has to find a way into their hearts, touching their emotions, making them laugh or cry and above all making them want to buy. In the end the listeners have to like you. They have to want to work with you. They have to like you better than the alternatives.

But be careful here. It is not enough for them to only want your organization emotionally. Even before you're appointed they will be thinking of how they are going to explain their choice to others. And it won't be enough to say, 'I just liked them'. A board of directors or a group of shareholders are going to want rational, persuasive evidence—the sort of evidence which will give the decision-maker permission to believe their own heart. So pitch on both levels: sell to the heart because that is where the real power lies, but give them sound rational reasons for trusting their gut instinct.

TIP
TIP

Evidence creates proof.

Experience tells me that most organizations have the evidence, but they usually have forgotten it or haven't bothered to use it. Keep files of case studies and examples; have them on computer and ready to bring into play as required.

TIP

We understood them.

I worked with a computer company pitching for a three million dollar account against five other suppliers. When the decision was given to my client, we went to the de-brief and asked the big question: 'Why did you choose us?' The client replied: 'You were the only supplier that we understood.' So spend time finding ways to keep it crisp, clean and simple. Make sure they understand all the key points. Don't baffle them with rubbish—say it well, but say it once.

TIP

Unmixing the senses.

If you are an advertising agency presenting a new television advertisement, then give some thought to separating the audio, visual and text components, so that the listeners can better appreciate the entire advertisement. If the music is strong, then talk first about what you needed the music to achieve. Darken the room and just play the music. Explain why you chose or created that particular track. Now talk about the visuals you needed to add to the music. Now play it again, but this time add the visuals. Discuss them. Now talk about the voice-over. Play it again and this time add the voice-over. Now play it all. If they're not sold by now, you need a new advertisement.

TIP

Poetic licence.

I worked with an advertising agency on a winning pitch in which the agency showed the client the 60-second television advertisement which it had created. Our creative director then darkened the room and ran the advertisement. It went for two and a half minutes! The rationale was that the client would not have fully appreciated the complexity of the advertisement if it had gone for only 60 seconds, so he made it longer.

TIP

Give them what they know.

The Sydney 2000 Olympic Bid presentation contained no new information for the IOC. They had heard it or read it all before. There were no shocks and no surprises, no last minute inducements to buy. The presentation itself was not designed to change everyone's minds, because that would have been impossible. It was written to confirm in the minds of the members supporting Sydney that they had made the right choice. And it was written to convert the undecided. No time was wasted trying to change the minds of those who would only ever vote for China.

Unless you know that the decision has already been made, the final presentation is not the time to try to change minds in the audience. You win the business before the presentation. And when you present you confirm in their minds that they made the right choice.

continued...

Often it is impossible to make a major change in someone's thinking in 30 minutes or two hours. There is simply too much to be done to achieve a turnaround. But you can work on someone over a few days or weeks and successfully change their mind.

TIP

Know the difference between creativity and gimmicks.

It is relatively easy to find gimmicks to glamorise your presentation. But it is much harder to find a creative tool which enhances the presentation theme, lifts it to a higher level and creates a change in the thinking or emotions of the listeners. Avoid gimmicks that are corny or, worse, that might insult the client.

TIP

The power of physical evidence.

It's one thing to tell a client that you have offices in San Francisco; it's another to show that client a photograph of the outside of the actual building with your office name engraved on a brass plaque. That's exactly what one of Australia's leading advertising agencies did to prove to a client that the office was a reality. Words last for seconds. Physical evidence lasts much longer.

TIP

The client will see things literally.

Too often an unqualified statement made by you in a pitch will be taken literally—with disastrous results. And it is too late to go back after the decision and say, 'But what I really meant was...' By the time the pitch comes around, your thinking may be so refined that it makes wonderful logic to you. Unfortunately the client does not have the benefit of your thinking—perhaps the client has not gone through the hours of brainstorming which your team has undergone. There will be a need to revisit where you last left the client's thinking, then bring them up to date by explaining the process you went through. Only then will the client be ready for your solution.

TIP

Clients have their own paradigms.

Put yourself into the client's seat throughout the process and the presentation. Look at every point in your presentation from the client's point of view. Fine-tune your language to reflect the client's values.

TIP

Talk like a member of the client team.

The feeling created in the pitch room should be one of a single team working together to discuss solutions. So speak as if you are sharing the problems: 'The challenge we face here is...' I often tell my team to imagine they are executives of the

continued...

potential client's company, presenting to the board or management team—not an outside consultant pointing out client mistakes and showing how only the consultant can fix it.

TIP

Show your willingness to own the client's problem.

The client wants you to take ownership of the problems, not comment and leave. They want to know that you will lift the hassles from their shoulders and fix them. And you'll be there for the duration.

TIP

This is going to be easy.

It's like going to the doctor. Who would you prefer to fix your health—the doctor who isn't at all sure if she can help because your problems are so bad, or the doctor who says, 'This is commonplace for me. I can fix you up in no time'? I know who I would go to. Be positive, bright, enthusiastic. Lift them, don't make them feel worse. Avoid telling the client that it will be hard to achieve what you are offering.

Rather than stand before the client with your brow knitted, stroking your chin, worried sick about the difficulty of the problem, why not show that they have chosen the right supplier here, because challenges like this are your bread and butter. Be the solution provider who does not have problems. That is why they will hire you.

TIP

Paint visual pictures for the audience, not only with aids, but by having them use their imagination. Theatre of the mind is very powerful. Each listener will imagine a scene in their own ways, with their own colours, people and positions. The images they create in their heads will be forceful.

TIP

Big is emotional.

If you're showing a video in a presentation, do it on a huge screen. Do it with plenty of volume. Don't use a small television and conservative sound. Make it bigger than life itself. Make the audience look up to the screen. Make them feel the music in their chests. Affect them.

TIP

The method reflects the claims.

If your claim is that you represent a professional organization, and yet you present like a raw amateur, the power of the visual and auditory images which you have created will far outweigh the words you have used. In short, the way the presentation is made reflects heavily all the claims stated by the presenters, from the first contact with the potential client to the final handshake. So decide on how you want to be perceived, and make sure that is how you really do come across.

TIP

Using the room.

Try presenting the different parts of your presentation from different parts of the presentation room. For example, the team leader starts the presentation in the middle at the front. The next speaker may speak from the left at the front. The next from the right. The next seated. The team leader goes back to the centre and sums up. By using this technique, the listener remembers more clearly the different parts of the talk, because you have provided visual links for each speaker by changing the background in each case. I have always wanted to try a presentation where each of four presenters speaks from a different wall in the room—and the audience turns their chairs around to face each new wall as each presenter begins.

TIP

Answer the right questions.

When taking a question from the client, if there is the slightest doubt in your mind about the intent of the query, check that you understand it before you attempt to answer it. Paraphrase the question back to the client.

TIP

Don't talk to the 'client', talk to individuals.

Effective communication is one-on-one. Many people think that when they are presenting in front of a group of individuals, they should talk to nobody in particular. Nothing

continued...

could be further from the truth. Focus on individuals in a presentation, use their names, address complete thoughts to targeted listeners, regardless of the size of the audience.

TIP

Use team language.

I strive to make sure that no pitch team member ever uses the 'you and us' language, like 'Your problem is XYZ, but we can fix it'. It wrongly polarizes the two parties. It says, 'This is not our problem, it's yours'. I ask my team to present as if they have already won the account and are facing the problems of the organization together. Use 'we' not 'you'.

TIP

One good idea on its own beats nine great ideas and one bad.

Don't put up 10 vague 'good' ideas. The danger is that they will remember the one which would not work. Put up three excellent ideas which you have checked with the client beforehand, so you know they work. The one bad idea is enough to prove that you do not understand the client's business. It shows that you have not been as thorough as you have claimed.

TIP

Putting price into perspective.

It's easy to become fixated over the effect of price on the outcome of a pitch. Too often the potential client stresses

continued...

that price will be the only determinant in deciding the winning supplier. Just as often, the potential suppliers get into the same rut. As a pitcher, you have to guess the lowest winning price point, because you do not always know how low your competitors might go. You might bid too low—and win the business only to find that you discounted far too much to win—or you might lose for the sake of a measly $1,000.

Price should not be pitched on its own. It must always be put into perspective. I always try to meet or exceed every demand in the client brief—going further than any other supplier might go—then I mention the price. Now it is in perspective.

The client's take-out is: 'We appointed this supplier because they met or exceeded our needs in every way—and then gave us a price which represented tremendous value.' Price on its own is not value.

Chapter 17

The Visuals and the Document

NOW YOU CAN HAVE A POWERFUL, convincing message in a convincing structure. It's time to add another dimension: visual aids.

Visual aids are essential for any presentation. Full stop. And there isn't a presentation I have seen that could not have been made better for the audience with visual aids.

'I hear and I forget, I see and I remember.' Chinese philosopher Sun Tzu was right. The visual aid taps into the sense of sight and the visual sense is far more powerful than the auditory. That said, there is too much reliance on visual aids as a panacea for poor presenting. It is true that visual aids add a new dimension to your presentation. They introduce another sense and they double or triple the effectiveness of the words. A strong video adds music, imagery, drama, colour and movement—all powerful motivators—bring art to a presentation and lift it to a new plane. However, they do not win presentations on their own.

Today's presenter certainly uses technology to its fullest through video, computer-driven visual aids and audio, but in the end people buy from people. And, at the risk of repetition, they most often buy from people they like.

That's why I recommend that organizations do not invest in product videos to be used by the sales force, but rather create powerful presenters who sell superbly, while using videos as visual aids only. A winning pitch is holistic. No single entity in the pitch should be remembered as being more powerful than another part. The whole event works. Without the presenter the visuals would lack focus and fact. Without the visuals the presenter would be less convincing.

So, once you have a structured presentation, add the visual aids. Select the visuals which best suit the tone, mood and the information you need to get across. A flipchart and a well-handled pen may be the very best for one group, a multi-screen audio-visual the best for another group.

The wonders of computer generated visuals will enhance presentations superbly, but be warned that the best, most colourful, most expensive slides in the world will not replace a strong communicator with a high level of intention. The role of visual aids is to help the presenter be even more effective.

TIP

> Build information.
>
> Don't present several ideas at once on your visual aid. Build information one step at a time by using an overlay on your overheads, or step by step reveal of key points on your 35mm slides, or the same technique on your computer-driven visuals. First show the parameters of the table, then add the first piece of information, then the second and so on, explaining each as you do it. That way you control the attention of the listeners.

TIP

> Give consideration to using a mix of visual aids—overheads, boards, flipcharts, slides, video, storyboards, product. Don't overdo it, but you can add variety by mixing the aids. During rehearsal, plan what aids you will be needing and have them prepared professionally.

TIP

> Client goes first.
>
> Don't fall for the easy mistake of putting your company logo prominently on the top of each visual. That's where you put the client's logo. Yours can go right down the bottom in a corner.

TIP

> Less is more.
>
> Buy one of the numerous booklets on how to design a slide and overhead. The rules are pretty simple: for information use five words per line, five lines per slide as a guideline. Invest in software and see what you can do beyond mechanical devices such as overheads and 35mm slide projectors.

THE DOCUMENT

The document which you leave behind should be a structural mirror of your presentation. It should use the same creative opening, the same order of information, the same summary and conclusion. If the client reads it—and there is often some doubt whether they do—then the document should reiterate the presentation the client saw earlier. The more it mirrors the presentation, the more it will reinforce your messages.

But the document is also the place for the additional detail for which you did not have time in the oral presentation. Don't make the mistake of putting this detail in the front of the document because it will become too cumbersome and long. Instead, create an addendum and fill that with the appendix materials. It means that the busy executive can just read the first half, and the analytical minds can find the detail in the back.

Your document should reflect the same tone and mood as your presentation. By that I mean the cover should be of a quality and style that matches the impression you want to give. Be wary of spending too much on quality and creativity because the client may sense that you waste money. But be equally careful not to spend too little, for fear the client thinks you don't care enough.

The document needs to be an integral part of the critical path leading to your presentation. It can take a large amount of time and office services for the document to be ready by the deadline.

TIP

> A fresh view.
>
> If you have the time, then get a professional writer to do a final rewrite. It is easy to get too close to the material when writing the document. The overall picture disappears and the main thrust is lost.

HOW CAN YOU MAKE IT DIFFERENT?

The document must show professionalism, whatever style it reflects. That means no photocopied pages. Give some thought to how your document will stand out from those of the competitor'. Can you make it landscape instead of portrait? Can it be A3 instead of A4? Bright red instead of white? Perfect bound? A two-volume document inside a cardboard case? I've delivered documents in wooden chests, aluminium cases, briefcases, cardboard folders and one document was printed a metre wide. At least it stood out.

Use break-out quotes and photographs. If you choose to include photographs of your team or organization, then make sure they are candid 'caught in the act' scenes of people actually doing something. Dress your entire company in client tee-shirts and put a group photograph in the front of the book. If the client sells hot chicken then have your team members eat chicken for the photograph. If the client sells cars, then sit your team members in and around some of their cars. Think about how you can make the document come alive.

Chapter 18

Polishing your Performance

REHEARSAL MAKES OR BREAKS A PRESENTATION. No rehearsal results in an unprofessional, confused transfer of information. Little rehearsal results in a mechanical, rigid display. Full rehearsal results in a natural presentation and gives the ability to add creativity. Every time you rehearse, you find something which could be done better. If you don't rehearse, you find all the mistakes during the presentation. And so does your prospective client! Rehearse in front of a mirror, to your partner, to your dog, and to business colleagues. Ideally rehearse again in the room in which you will present. It may not always be possible, but you won't know unless you ask. The best advertising agencies, for example, when pitching for a major new account, will always ask if they can have access to the room before the presentation. Set it up the way you want it, check that the visual aids can be seen from every chair, test the PA, test the overhead so you know where to switch it on and how to focus it, make sure there are spare bulbs for the equipment, check the light switches, test for sound, look for distracting windows, pot plants, noises and doors. Practise delivering your presentation to the empty chairs, improving your eye contact, movement and gestures. Get to know the room until you feel you own the space.

Three team rehearsals are a minimum for any pitch, and individual team members should be rehearsing in between. You'll need at least a walk-through, a rehearsal and a dress rehearsal, plus each team member will be responsible for rehearsing their own pieces on their own.

The first rehearsal is the walk-through. It normally occurs two to three weeks before the presentation. Sit around the table and walk through the presentation from beginning to end, with each person saying what they will say and do. Check that each person's role is understood and that no overlaps are occurring. Don't bother with visual aids at this point. Don't even bother deciding how you will present it.

Now talk it through again, looking for waste. Discuss what visual aids will work best with this audience, given the tone and mood you wish to create. Plan what each person will do by the next rehearsal. The venue needs to checked to make sure that nothing has changed since your first visit. Do you know exactly what equipment will be provided?

In a $40 million dollar winning pitch that we coached, we dismantled the client boardroom table—it was 25 feet (some six metres) long—and took the centre pieces out of it to make a more intimate room. What can you do to make the room more suitable? If you have many items to display in the presentation and there are no suitable walls, then have some demountable walls made up. Don't accept that you have to put up with a bad room. Strive to get it perfect.

The second run-through will occur up to a week before the presentation. By now you will have your visual aids either finished or written out on pieces of A4 paper or on a flipchart. For this presentation, work through each segment without comment, then critique it at the end of each part. So while one person presents a piece, the rest will sit in silence and make notes. Stand up or sit down as you will in the presentation. Read from your notes if necessary. Start to plan the transitions from one speaker to the next. Plan how you will handle the visual aids.

Cross-check everything against the objective. Chop any extraneous material out of the pitch. Set yourself a 'fun' objective to cut it by a third. Look out for repetition and vary the pace. Start to think about the tone and how that tone will affect the audience.

Is the blend of analytical, expressive and direct styles right for this audience? Is it going to be too conservative, too casual? Is the blend of visual aids appropriate? Check that the creative hook is there. Where is the flair and colour, and what will make it memorable? What are the questions that will be answered, and how will they be answered?

Set in place some objectives for each person to achieve between this run-through and the final rehearsal. The visual aids must be finished. Each person will have to be up to speed on their own parts.

Send your team away to rehearse their your presentation. Suggest that team members rehearse with in pairs.

The final rehearsal should occur early enough before the presentation to allow final changes and, more importantly, to provide sufficient 'quiet time' for each presenter to relax and get their own act together. If the presentation is early in the morning I suggest that you rehearse from 9 am the day before.

If it is to happen late in the afternoon, then the latest it should be held is at 7 am that morning.

You'll judge when to hold the final rehearsal based on how far you have progressed. Some pitches are easy to plan, but in others the solution is not even apparent until hours before the pitch. Ideally the rehearsal will be held in the room in which you will hold the actual presentation. But experience shows that will not always be possible, so set up your own room to mirror exactly the presentation room. Mark the walls with tape to show where the light switches will be. Place the table in the same position, put the screen in place.

I like to rehearse the final presentation in front of an audience of workmates who have not been involved. Get them to role-play the individuals. Have them ask the tough questions. Have them be hypercritical. Make sure contact exists between each presenter and each client. Go back to basics. Are we addressing key thoughts to key people? Place the 'client' in the seat they will be in. Use eye contact appropriate to the roles of each in the client team. In other words, if there is only one decision-maker, then give that person 60% to 70% of the eye contact. If others are key influencers, then give them the appropriate amount also. If you have an influencer who is a specialist in, say finance, then make sure that person gets eye contact during that subject.

When you have finished the rehearsal, ask the audience to critique, but first ask them this question: 'What are the one, two or three things that you will walk away from this presentation with?' Make sure that the answers match up with your expectations.

Rehearsals can be staged after 5 pm and on weekends. The winners are the suppliers which put in the *extra* effort. They are not concerned about rehearsing one more time late at night or on a Sunday. It is expected by management and never questioned by the presentation team.

Here are some tips as used by the experts.

TIP

Building mock people.

We often create cardboard cutouts of the clients and sit them in the room for rehearsal. Stick their photographs

continued...

where the faces are. If you don't want to go to that length, put name tags on the table and present to them.

TIP

Check that everyone can see your visual aids.

Once you have gained access to the final presentation room, lay out the chairs in the positions that you think best, and then draw an imaginary line between each chair and the visual aids you will be using. Make certain that everyone on the client side can see the visuals. During the presentation, your team may have to push its chairs back from the table to allow this to happen.

TIP

Rehearsing is time well spent.

Don't get disillusioned by the time you spend rehearsing. It is seldom wasted. I find that the primary reason that people do not want to rehearse is that they will find out sooner that they are not ready! And they don't want to find that out in front of their peers, so instead they rely on blind optimism in the hope that 'it will be alright on the day'. It never is. The value of going through the process may not be seen on the surface but, even if you spend weeks analysing and then finally rejecting ideas and concepts, the worth of having gone through the process will be seen in the finished product.

TIP

Make it easy for the client to know your name.

Prepare an 'order of presenters' sheet for each member of the audience and put each person's name on the top. Then list the order of your team's presenters. Don't make it an agenda, just a list of speakers with their names and titles. Put one sheet in front of the chair in which you wish that person to sit. People will be flattered by the attention to detail and they will find it easier to follow the flow of the presentation.

TIP

Careful of sounding overconfident.

Avoid saying: 'If we get the business...' Instead, use language like: 'What we will be doing is...' Do not sound overconfident, but don't highlight that you haven't won. Constantly reminding the listeners that you are only one choice of several works against your winning.

TIP

One solution or more.

Sometimes there are more possible solutions than just one. You haven't been able to get to the client, or they don't know which one is right either. The best way to present the options is first to present the criteria for judging the best solution. Then present the worst match, then the next, and finally the best solution—according to the criteria.

TIP

> Avoid playback.
>
> Too often I see bidders begin their pitch by playing back, word for word, the client's own briefing. Tell them something they don't know! By all means give them your interpretation of their brief (especially if you are the first team presenting to them in a line-up of competitors), but if you are the last team to present, you can find better things to do than repeat a brief which others have doubtless already repeated to them. The same is true of any information which you feel other competitors may have already presented to them. If your team is the fifth bidder to present, you will bore the client by repeating something they have heard four times before.

TIP

> Synergy.
>
> Each part of your presentation must add to, build on, or be in synergy with the rest. In an advertising pitch the creative must be in tune with the strategy. In a computer pitch the solution must mirror the emphasis of the problem.

TIP

> Adjust the voice for contact.
>
> During rehearsal, spend time getting the volume right for the audience. The right volume is that which makes contact. It sounds right to the listener—not too loud, not too quiet—
>
> *continued...*

just right for contact. Check with the listeners during rehearsal to make sure your voice is making contact. Check whether you modulate to the volume and pace to emphasize and create an effect. Are you making contact?

TIP

Why am I showing this slide?

Try not to show slides for the sake of showing slides. As each slide goes up during rehearsal, ask yourself what point you wish to make by showing this slide. Make sure there is a comment to be made that will interest the client. If you are showing research, for example, then what is the take-out? What is the audience going to do as a result of seeing that slide? Will they change their thinking? Will they be different? If the answer is no, then think about getting rid of the slide entirely.

TIP

Keep a running checklist.

Throughout the planning, writing and rehearsal process keep your team on track by having a checklist available for each presenter, as well as for those in the team who may not actually be present but are playing a role in building the case. The checklist should have:

+ the name of the presenter;

+ the part they will play in the pitch;

+ the outcome sought from the listeners;

continued...

> ✦ key points to be made; and
>
> ✦ evidence to be used.
>
> Use the sheets during rehearsals to make sure each person

A FINAL RECAP

So let's look once again at the process of preparing to present. The first step is audience analysis—and it is a probably the most important step. If you get it right, then the rest is much easier to plan and prepare. If you get it wrong, then you are risking your business.

The second step is objective setting—and not only is it critical to have an attainable objective, but it will help you focus your attention before and during the presentation. You cannot set a specific objective until you know the audience, its needs and abilities.

The third step is persuasive information—to assemble the facts, figures and evidence which will get that specific audience to reach your specific objective. You cannot collect the right information until you know what the audience needs and what your objective is.

Step four is structure—to choose an appropriate organizational flow for your presentation. And the right structure will depend on the audience, the objective and the amount and style of information collected.

Step five is visual aids—to plan and create the right number of the right kind of visual aids to add emphasis, clarity, focus, and sometimes fun, to your presentation. The visual aids chosen will be dependent on the audience, the objective, the information and the structure.

At this point you have an appropriately structured, persuasive presentation, tailored to get a specific audience to reach your specific objective and assisted by appropriate visual aids. Now you can start the process of rehearsal.

Step six is a read-through—with a difference. Put yourself in the shoes of the decision-makers in your audience. Get into their mind-set and then read your script or notes through section by section. Every now and then, usually at the bottom of a page, stop and say, 'So what?' Ask yourself if you would understand what that section meant and as the decision-maker, would you be convinced? If you find passages that are irrelevant, then either make them relevant or cut them out. You should be able to discard up to 30% of a loosely worded presentation.

Step seven is rehearsal. Do it in the shower, in your car, in a room, in front of your peers, in the actual room. Test everything. Ask the tough questions and answer them. Don't neglect rehearsal.

Step eight is delivery—but there is still one more step if you want to keep on improving.

Step nine is the debrief. Immediately after your presentation think about the things which worked, and the things which did not. Did you reach your objective? Did you read the audience well? Did you handle every question comfortably and considerately? Make a note of the strengths and weaknesses of your team's presentation and attach the notes to your scripts. File them away for next time.

Chapter 19

Tips on Delivery

T HE LIBRARIES ARE FULL OF BOOKS on public speaking and presenting. Buy one and read it. Here are some key points on delivery, some of which you may not find elsewhere.

TIP

Seating the client.

Should we mix the client up with our own team? Should they sit at one end and you sit at the other? The answer is that it depends. The mandatories are that the client must be able to see the visual aids. The client should be close to the presenter, not the length of a table away (but perhaps the width away instead). The seating should reflect the tone you want to achieve in the room. Try sitting the four or five clients along one side of the table. Sit your team around one end. Let the presenter speak from across the table. It doesn't matter if your own people have lousy seats, but it is critical that the client team gets the dress circle.

TIP

A presentation is a moving feast.

A presentation is flexible. It changes as it proceeds because, as it flows, it affects the audience. If, halfway through, you discover the idea that you were going to present is no longer applicable or suitable, just drop it. Sound planning will have warned you that it might happen and with good planning you will have an alternative. Don't lock yourself into inevitable disaster. If the presentation is not going right, change it. Don't leave a creative idea in if it stinks. It casts doubt on the quality of your thinking.

Be yourself.

A San Francisco trainer Jim Bartlett once taught me four hip-pocket rules for presenting: It's OK! So what? Be yourself and have fun.

◆ It's OK—it takes the listeners much longer to wake up to the fact that you have lost your place. Just pause and walk back to your notes then keep going—95% of mistakes made by presenters are not noticed by the audience, until the presenter points them out.

◆ So what?—if you can't fix something, just go on without it. If the bulb blows, the flipchart is missing, you forget a section of your speech, don't worry. If you can't fix it, just keep rolling. Chances are the audience will never notice. But they will if you make an issue out of it!

◆ Be yourself—don't try to be someone you're not. If you make a mistake, who cares? Just pause and keep going. Listeners want you to succeed. They are usually on your side. Relax and be natural.

◆ Have fun—a fun presentation is never boring. Find ways to introduce a little humour. Lighten up a little! You will feel better and the audience will enjoy itself more.

Love your product.

Take care how you handle things in your presentation, because the way you treat them reflects the degree of respect you have for them. If you are picking up an artist's impression which your team has created for the client, do so by the edges. Treat it with love and respect. It is after all so important that you are showing it to the client. When you have shown it, place it down carefully, don't toss it aside.

If you are showing a creative design, don't stand away from it and point. Draw it to you and become part of it. Hold it close to your face and point out the highlights with care. Caress it because often it is the sum total of what you offer. It is the finished product.

TIP

Using first names.

If you have the right level of rapport with the audience (and you should know if you do by now), use the clients' first names in the presentation. However, if a very senior person is sitting in and you haven't had the chance to meet that person, find out from someone who knows just how they expect to be addressed.

TIP

It's never too late to learn.

You can still keep learning, even in the presentation itself. Use planned questions to ascertain the thinking of individuals. Be totally aware of the reactions of each listener to different parts of your presentation. Watch how listeners react with each other in the room and see if that reaction matches your own research.

TIP

Changing speech to conversation.

It is a very common occurrence to change your whole demeanour when you start to present. The warmth and charisma which you showed when chatting one-on-one disappears in a blaze of nervous energy when you stand to present. You become stilted, overly formal, loud, precise—all aspects of communication which do little to build rapport.

The situation worsens when the presenter is also reading from a speech. One technique which may help is to add a few tiny, almost meaningless words to the front of each sentence. Here are two examples:

Stilted version: 'We at XYZ company believe your problem is complex, but the solution is achievable.'

Conversational version: 'You know, it's interesting, we believe your problem is complex, but the solution is achievable.'

or

Stilted version: 'The options available to your organization include X, Y and Z.'

Conversational version: 'The fact is, the options available to your organization include X, Y and Z.'

The very act of standing up can be enough to change some people's speech into a stilted, formal, loud style. Try rehearsing sitting down. Note how the voice becomes more relaxed and conversational, then stand up and maintain the same tone. The difference can be dramatic.

TIP

> Controlling the tone.
>
> You have the power to control the tone and mood of the room. Think about the size of your gestures, the volume of your voice, the speed and amount of movement. Small gestures, a quiet voice and little movement create a conservative impression. Large fast gestures, a booming voice and violent fast movements create a dynamic environment. You can affect the impression.

OVERCOMING NERVES

Surveys suggest that around 85% of people put the fear of presenting in their top three fears and, of that number, half put it above death itself. A bad case of nerves before, at the beginning of or during a major presentation can be the difference between success and failure, between a career boost or the unemployment line.

So what causes nerves?

Experts will tell you that nerves are caused by a flood of adrenalin throughout the body, stemming from an inbuilt need to fight or flee from danger. That's interesting, but not necessarily helpful.

One reason for nervousness is the fact that you haven't done it before or certainly not often enough. It is no different from climbing into a car for the first time—if you haven't done it before you will certainly be nervous.

The starting point in dealing with nerves is to appreciate that the difference between a dynamic presenter and a distracted ditherer is *focus*. The ability to focus on one's audience and objective in a presentation is a huge plus. It's almost impossible to focus on an objective if your mind is filled with distractions. With poor preparation you are consciously or subconsciously distracted by a host of 'what ifs?' and 'am Is?' including:

◆ 'What if the audience doesn't like what I'm going to say?'

◆ 'What if they ask a question I can't answer?'

◆ 'What if they find me lacking?'

◆ 'What if I make a goat of myself?'

◆ 'Am I holding my hands correctly?'

◆ 'Am I standing correctly?'

◆ 'Am I speaking loudly enough, clearly enough?'

◆ 'Am I using this projector correctly?'

One key to overcoming nerves is to end these distracting thoughts. Once they are no longer spinning around inside your head, it's easier to focus on winning the business. Most of the 'what if?' and 'am I?' type questions are caused by your not really being sure of yourself, and what you are like as a presenter. So find out. Get some help from an expert. As a truly nervous presenter your mind can be filled with a buzz of distractions to the point where everything becomes fuzzy and only the notes keep you on track.

But a trained presenter knows what to do with the hands, how to use the slide or overhead projector, how to modulate the voice, where to look, what to say and what not to say. The prepared presenter knows a lot about the listeners and what they want to hear, knows the answers to the rough questions and has evidence to prove the answers, and knows who the decision-makers are in the audience.

Solid audience analysis preparation and rehearsal will overcome a host of distractions. And by answering the distracting questions in advance, your mind is cleared and free to focus on the listeners and your objective.

If you're still nervous, then think of the physical things that have happened to your body as the presentation has drawn near. Are you breathing normally? Nervousness tends to shut down the body. You move less, breathe less, talk less. None of these things help you present dynamically.

Top presenters use a variety of means to prepare themselves for their presentation or speech. Here are some that I use:

✦ Sit quietly, close the eyes, and run a mental checklist of everything to do with the presentation. 'Have I covered the points?' Tell yourself: 'Yes, I can forget about that.'

As each item is mentally checked off you no longer need to worry about it. I advise any pitch team to allow a few hours for individuals to have some quiet time between the last rehearsal and the actual presentation.

✦ Rehearse. Get into the presentation room. Try out the equipment, practise the words, pace the floor, get used to the microphone or lectern, switch the overhead on and off, adjust the lights until it becomes natural and you don't have to think about it.

✦ Tense your upper stomach muscles for 30 seconds, then relax. This helps loosen the muscles which drive the voice.

Some presenters achieve the same by leaning with arms stretched ahead and hands pushed against a wall.

✦ Get rid of excess energy by screaming. This works by loosening up the voice box, but can unnerve your fellow team members, and the client.

✦ Reiterate the objective of the presentation and focus on it.

✦ Visualize yourself succeeding and picture the audience responding positively.

✦ Talk to individuals in the client team, not to the whole group. This is the natural thing to do. As business people we can all speak naturally to individuals. But speaking to the group as a whole is not natural.

All of these techniques work. Some work for one presenter, some for others. It's a matter of trying each to find the one that best suits you. But, in the end, it is the simple answer which is right—and the hardest to do. You have to get some help. You have to prepare. You have to know your stuff. You have to rehearse. And you have to keep your attention on the listeners and your objective.

TIP

Proving the point

The advertising executive leaned over the table to the prospect and said: 'You're probably sitting there thinking that this is the last time you will see me. I'll land the account then pass you down to someone in the company. I thought about this and asked myself: "How can I convince you that this is not the case?" Here is what I did.'

continued...

He leaned down and pulled a typed letter from his briefcase and read it to the client. 'I pledge to make myself available at any time night or day for the next three years. My telephone numbers at home and work are...' Picking up a pen he signed it with a flourish and handed it over the table. 'I can't be more serious than that, can I?'

TIP

Coffee first.

If you can get the presentation to be held at your own offices, or at a venue of your choice, then organize coffee first. There are two good reasons why. First, most client executives will arrive at different times, so it gives the early arrivers something to do while the others are travelling. Secondly, and much more importantly, it gives everybody on your team the chance to meet the individuals on the client team, to shake their hands, to use their names, and to build rapport by discussing interesting non-business topics.

Serve the coffee in a different room. If you serve it in the presentation room then it is difficult to get a crisp start to your presentation. More often than not, everybody drinks their coffee and, when the start of the presentation is signalled, someone will reach for another cup. Worse, from a physical point of view, the definition of the start of the presentation is hampered by the fact that everybody is already seated in their presentation position, so nothing physical changes.

continued...

I always recommend serving coffee in the anteroom. Then, when everyone has arrived and been introduced, your presentation team members usher their guests through to the presentation room and seat them where you want them to end up.

TIP

Time is money.

Finish in one hour if they allow 90 minutes. Ninety minutes if they allow two hours. At the start of your presentation tell them how long you will be talking for and how long you have allowed for questions. The old rule says that your last rehearsal will be 20% shorter than the actual presentation.

TIP

Gee, this is great!

During the pitch, do not write or pass notes to each other. It signals that you are not as prepared as you should have been. And it shows that the person speaking is not gaining 100% of your attention. Avoid any signs of boredom and disinterest, like yawning, looking around, doodling. Never correct mistakes or talk over a fellow team member. Concentrate only on the presenter. Show support and agreement.

TIP

Monitor the listeners.

While making sure you are watching your presenter, also keep an eye on the members of the audience. Check how they are reacting. Look for positive communication indicators, such as leaning forward, nodding, smiling, building on comments, taking appropriate notes. Look also for the indicators which are not so positive, like a queried look, folded arms and legs, inappropriate note taking, yawning, disinterest. If somebody is obviously bored or bewildered, tactfully ask if you can help: 'You look a little puzzled, Bob. Can I help in any way?'

TIP

Controlling questions.

As a rule, have client questions fielded by the team leader. They can take the query, play it back to make sure it is the 'real question', and direct it to the team member best able to give the right answer. You control the process, and you can provide time for the answerer to collect their thoughts.

TIP

Clear your space.

While you are presenting the room is yours. Fill it with your visuals, charts, boards and equipment. But once you have finished, clear your space for the next presenter. They should be able to step into a clear area in which only the aids

continued...

needed for the pitch remain. A common mistake which highlights lack of rehearsal and teamwork is one presenter leaving their visuals up after that segment is over. The listener sees a clutter of mixed messages, no longer relevant to the point being made.

TIP

Pitch to their values.

Align your words to their values, not your own. Talk less about what you believe in and more about their own values. Make sure your presentation matches their needs but make certain it doesn't clash with their values.

TIP

Do not criticize and do not preach.

Never in a presentation do we criticize the client for anything. Never.

I may have fun at the expense of my family and my friends when I'm in a situation where that sort of thing is understood. But woe betide if a stranger tries to criticize my family in front of me. In the same way, it is alright for a client to speak badly about their own organization, but they do not want to hear it from others—especially strangers.

A guaranteed pitch-losing strategy is to stand before the client management in the presentation and tell them what

continued...

they are doing wrong. Don't talk about problems or mistakes. Talk about challenges and opportunities. Look forward, not back. Clients will hire you because you have shown them the light at the end of the tunnel, not because you reminded them of how badly they have done.

TIP

Presenting media campaigns.

If you are a member of an advertising agency which is presenting a media campaign to a client, ask the listeners to imagine they are members of the target audience. Walk the listeners through a 'day in the life' of that person, from when they get up and switch on the radio, pick up the morning paper, drive to work (or take public transport). The words go something like this: 'Ted, as a member of your product's target market, you will probably listen to 2GE radio in the morning. This campaign will include ads during the breakfast program. You will travel to work by car, and the advertising will continue on your car radio, and also on billboards leading into the city. You may pick up a motoring magazine at lunchtime, and again you will see advertisements for this product. As you drive home, we will be advertising on drive-time radio, and when you turn on your favourite television programs at night, we will have advertisements on Channels X and Y.'

This technique—of having clients imagine they are the target market—ensures that they 'feel' how effective a media campaign will be.

TIP

Watch out for the bad egg.

If you are presenting three alternatives to a potential client, think carefully about each alternative. If one idea is obviously unworkable, it will cast doubt on the quality of your thinking —thus affecting the reception given to your other ideas. Drop it out.

TIP

It's already in their hearts—just tap into it.

Motivation comes from within. Inspirational language is not motivational unless the particular recipient is ready to receive it. Shouting words at someone will not motivate them, unless you strike a chord within. Striking that chord is secondary to finding the chord in the first place.

Great advertising does not put new feelings into people. It simply taps existing feelings and ideas that lie, sometimes dormant, in people. So it is with great presenters. Martin Luther King has been credited with extraordinary presentation ability, but his great skill was undoubtedly in tapping into the feelings that existed in the hearts of not only African-Americans, but many other people as well.

Take that objective into a business presentation. Find the feelings that are latent in the audience. Tap into them, release them and give them evidence that proves what you say is true. That's the secret of a winning presentation.

Chapter 20

After the Presentation

THE WHISTLE GOES WHEN THE PRESENTATION ENDS.

Never stop pitching. Find reasons to go back to the client after the presentation. If the client asks a question which cannot be fully dealt with during the pitch, get back to them in writing within 24 hours. If they build on one of your ideas by suggesting another option, check that option out within 24 hours and get back to them. For example, during the presentation the client might ask if you investigated a particular alternative strategy or concept. Deal with it in the meeting, but also get back to the client in writing the next day. Even when the contract is signed, you keep on selling because there is more business to be won from this client—or from people that the client will talk to. Find ways to keep communication going beyond the presentation.

If at the end of your presentation you get no questions, you're probably in deep trouble.

If, however, the potential client has a lot of specific questions, things are looking good. The more specific they are, the better you are looking.

How you handle those post-pitch questions could decide the viability of the account in the short and long-term. The emotional argument is to agree to the small requests which the client makes, because you really want the account (after all, you've been pitching it for weeks and the investment in time, effort and money is considerable). But this is the time for brave thinking. While emotionally it is not a time to be arguing with the potential clients, watch the details. They can make the difference between a workable, mutually beneficial relationship and a frustrating, damaging account which harms the organization.

Whatever else you may do, don't focus on the end of your presentation as being the end of your pitch. Keep your team focused on winning the business, and that means not stopping until you have been given the business. Keep on pitching until you have been told you've lost. Then keep on pitching until you know it's true. Find ways to give the client added value after the presentation has ended, hours after, days after, weeks after—whatever it takes to show the client how keen you are, how hungry you are.

If you've won the account the communication from the client usually continues. If there is no contact after the pitch, then you were either so thorough that every query was answered in the presentation or document, or it is more likely that they are talking to a competitor. Try to keep talking to the client after the pitch. Ask if they need more, offer to provide extra detail, try to get them to commit to a next step. Remember that if they're not talking to you, they are probably talking to your competitors.

If the presentation is important enough, it's expected that you will wheel out the appropriate level of big gun to say a few words—your CEO, chairperson, divisional head. But, as I've pointed out before, be very aware that the client perception is often that this person is there out of sufferance—and will never be seen again. Ensure that your top person maintains client contact after the pitch, out of courtesy to some extent, but also to show that the commitment goes right to the top, and is ongoing.

TIP

> Why not video your presentation?
>
> Why not make a lasting impression with the client by videoing your final rehearsal and giving the client a copy after the presentation, so they can refresh themselves with your pitch later. This means that your message can be given a life beyond the actual presentation. Instead of the client having to read your submission or a take-out, they can watch your presentation again, with all its colour, sound and movement.

Pray for a decision within two weeks because, if there is no contact for two weeks, something bad has happened. Dead silence is not something that occurs between partners. I've tried the theory again and again and it seems to be true more often that not that, if the rules of the pitch do not allow a long decision time, then after two weeks of silence the business is probably gone. There is no doubt that as time passes the power of the presentation dissipates. The emotion leaves and only the logic remains. Sometimes it is not enough. So find ways to keep contact going. A sure winning signal is when the client comes back after the presentation and starts checking minor details. The more minor they are, the more likely you are to have won.

Chapter 21

Some thoughts for the other side of the table

THE PITCH is now a solid part of business life. Advertising agencies, computer companies, construction companies, banks and other financial institutions, financiers, law firms, accountancy practices—all professional organizations pitch for business— collectively to hundreds of thousands of clients around the world. I feel strongly that both the pitchers and the potential clients have a responsibility to each other. I have written extensively about how pitchers should handle their task, but little has been written about the responsibilities of the potential clients.

Imagine if a very large organization was facing a multi-million dollar court case in three months' time. Instead of talking to its legal company, it instead provided the legal brief to 10 law firms and sought their solutions to the problem, including the strategy and approaches for solving the legal dilemma. Then after all the presentations have been made, it accepted only one legal firm to handle the project.

Hard to imagine? To a legal firm yes, but not to an advertising agency, because that is exactly what happens every day in the advertising industry. Agencies provide thousands—sometimes hundreds of thousands—of dollars worth of advice, strategy, research and creativity on the off-chance of winning an account.

And the same is true for public relations, management consultants and many other 'consulting' organizations.

It is not unheard of for advertising agencies to spend jointly in excess of one million dollars pitching for a large piece of business. Some agencies have each spent in excess of $300,000 to $400,000 trying to win one account.

The agency world is now in a vicious circle which, to some degree, it has created itself. It must keep pitching business because revenue is decreasing while costs rise. As a result, some agencies will play the game according to any rules which the client might set. If an agency refuses to play, then it doesn't get the business. And there always seems to be one or more agencies who will do what the client wants to win the business.

Things which some potential clients have done, which I believe range from stupid to unethical, include:

✦ Issuing a brief then denying the potential suppliers access to key executives within the organization can occur. The crazy expectation is that the bidders will understand in hours or days what the company has taken years to know. This results in bidders being forced to make sometimes wild assumptions and thus the quality of the solutions is sometimes way off course. The organization seeking to appoint a supplier suffers by not getting accurate solutions and often one supplier is appointed because it 'fluked' the right solution, regardless of the fact that it could never do it again.

✦ I have seen some clients issue a brief then refuse to share available research and other information. Limiting information only results in both parties suffering.

✦ Calling a pitch which is not really a pitch at all can happen. This is only an exercise to get some new ideas or to 'keep the current supplier on its toes'. This practice, despite being dishonest, does occur, and the decision-makers have absolutely no intention of ever changing suppliers. The bidders could spend weeks and hundreds of thousands of dollars never knowing that the pitch is not actually 'on'.

PITCH DOCTOR

✦ The extension of this practice is to pay a token sum to all suppliers presenting, then demand rights to the strategies, ideas and creative work presented. It ends any legal concerns about who owns what at the end of the pitch, but strategies, research results and creative work which have been developed are bought for a fraction of their real worth.

✦ There is a practice by which a potential client will, at a whim, add a few more suppliers to the list, knowing that they will not have a chance of winning. The bidders will still spend days, if not weeks, focusing on the client problems and preparing, sometimes at a huge cost, the presentations. Ethically, they should not be asked to pitch if they have no opportunity to win.

✦ If you were to hire a new employee, you would certainly talk to that person's former employers. I am amazed that major suppliers can be hired without checking that supplier's other customers and former customers. The easiest way to check out the credentials of a supplier is to ring its clients—all its clients—and ask for an honest appraisal of the relationship, the service, the quality, the level of thinking, the accounting and administrative practices.

✦ Issuing a brief then changing it part-way through the pitch process also happens. Sometimes a supplier might try to manipulate a change in the brief to suit its own purpose. The client should refuse to change the brief midstream for the benefit of one supplier.

✦ Not having thought through the brief is a common problem. A recent brief for an account worth many millions of dollars was a page and a half long. Client contact was forbidden after the brief, so the only information available to the supplier companies was contained in those few words.

✦ Some suppliers may be favoured over others, by providing access or information which others cannot get.

✦ The pitch process can be used to solve a marketing or distribution problem, but the business never awarded.

✦ Clients may decide on a review based on there being a new marketing director—a new broom—rather than taking time to establish clear objective reasons for a review. The pitch process is an expensive one for everybody concerned. The bidders must spend days, weeks or months and so must the client. A review of the current supplier might just save other suppliers a lot of time and effort.

The pitch game is a great game. Played well it will stretch the suppliers and deliver new heights of creativity, thinking and effort. Both sides play an equally important part in the game and both have a responsibility to play fairly. It is fine to play tough, but it should always be fair!

CONCLUSION

Pitching is the most exciting, most rewarding, most work-intensive, most demotivating, most challenging, most frustrating, most intangible part of business life. It is also the future. The choice is yours—embrace the art of pitching or let others win the business. Become expert. Have pitching methodology inculcated through your organization. Lower the odds, increase your chances. It could be worth millions!

INDEX